Creeksailor
Ready About On The River Blackwater

Exploring the creeks, ditches and shoals in a small boat

By Tony Smith

Smaller Boat

Front cover picture; Goldhanger Creek by M Newport
Back cover picture; Goldhanger Creek at low water by T Smith

ISBN No 978-0-9569030-0-6
First published July 2011
Reprinted November 2011
Published by Smaller Boat Publications 2B Greenleyes, Allens Green, Sawbridgeworth, Herts,
CM21 0LR
Copyright photographs and text © Tony Smith 2011

Note: The accompanying map includes some of the more obvious barge docks and former docks,
red hills and beaches. Regarding former barge docks, it is reasonable to assume that any suitable area
beside a farm field may well have been frequented.

This book is for general interest only and not for navigational purposes.

Names, places and features change, so please do make your own checks using proper navigational
charts before visiting any of the places mentioned.

Printed and bound in England

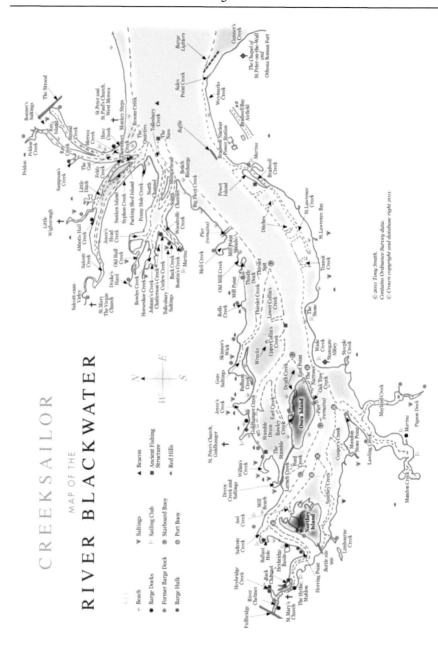

CREEKSAILOR

MAP OF THE

RIVER BLACKWATER

© 2011 Tony Smith.
Contains Ordnance Survey data.
© Crown copyright and database right 2011.

Contents

Map		3
Foreword		5
Introduction		6
1.	A Small-Boat Sailor's Haven	7
2.	Across The Stumble	13
3.	Smugglers And Jupiter	23
4.	Wild And Wonderful Saltings	35
5.	To Maldon	46
6.	Creek Harvest	59
7.	In Search Of The Red Hills	74
8.	Lawling, Mayland, Mundon and Steeple Creek	80
9.	Goldhanger Creek	88
10.	Northey Island, Limbourne and Awl Creek	93
11.	St Lawrence Bay Ditches	100
12.	Shoals	105
13.	A Creeksailor's Tool Kit	109
14.	The Gun Punt	115
15.	Traditional Sailmaking	119
16.	Traditional Boatbuilding	122
17.	Small-Boat Sailors	126
18.	Creeks Of The River Blackwater	134
	Acknowledgements	146
	Bibliography and Further Reading	147

Foreword

Looking back from my 84th year, many events stand out. One among them was my first sail down the glorious River Blackwater. Fortunately, it was a perfect day, with an afternoon tide, and the whole river teemed with life afloat and on the beaches. Once through the narrows between Osea Island and the Stansgate shore, a wide vista opened up before us to reveal the busy island town of West Mersea to the north and the lonely marshes to the south.

Over the following months and years, I realised that there were many smaller, attractive creeks and potential anchorages on either hand to make this an ideal estuary for the small-boat sailor.

Just why the modest little River Blackwater, which winds through the Essex countryside, should open up into such a wide estuary is a mystery. One possible explanation is that many moons ago, the River Thames drained into the North Sea this way and was cut off by advancing ice that reached far inland during the ice age.

Nevertheless, whatever quirk of nature produced it, this magnificent area is there to be enjoyed afloat or on land, and all visitors will vastly boost that enjoyment if they take along this meticulous account of each and every nook and cranny.

Charles Stock
Gaff-cutter *Shoal Waters*

Introduction

This pocket-size book is an account of cruising adventures and observations in and around the River Blackwater, or The Pant, as it was once known. It is in part an answer to questions raised many years ago when, as a small boy, I would often play on the beaches of Essex. It was from here that a fire of inquisitiveness was ignited by sheer wonderment at the sight seen offshore; of a ship adorned in tanned sails, slowly but surely edging its way along the coast and often coming from an area to the south-west where two utterly alien and strange towers jutted up from a distant land that lay beyond a hazy horizon. The towers were, of course, Bradwell power station, and the ships with tanned sails Thames spritsail barges. But it would be years later as an adult that I would get answers to what lay beyond those towers.

The aim of this book is to convey to the reader some of those answers found through the joy and delight of small-boat sailing in the quieter lesser-known areas of the river, too often neglected or avoided by far larger craft. The book also endeavours to rekindle memories of past maritime traditions, both on land and on water, while also retelling many of the experiences I have enjoyed on board my 14 foot lugsail dinghy and my converted 16 foot gaff cutter moored at Goldhanger Creek. Much has been written about this river previously, but little to wet the appetite of the shoal draft pocket-cruiser owner or dinghy sailor. I hope, too, that this little book will prove of interest not only to those sailors who appreciate the unique qualities of the Blackwater estuary but also to all those with a genuine love of this part of Essex.

Of all the harbours and havens on the East Coast, it is difficult to escape the lure of the Blackwater, with its traditional mix of farming, fishing and sailing that seems to cast an alluring spell on all who visit its shores.

Tony Smith
Creeksailor

*"The lonely beaches are too remote for anyone but the serious
hiker, but they can be reached in a small boat"*

Chapter One

A Small-Boat Sailor's Haven

Looking down river from East Point, Osea.

THE RIVER BLACKWATER has a wide, inviting entrance of
approximately one-and-a-half miles across from Sales Point on the south
shore to Mersea Island on its northern edge. From there to the barge-lined
Hythe Quay at Maldon is a distance of about ten miles. With such a large
expanse of water, the Blackwater provides fantastic sailing.

The river and its creeks and ditches are dotted with idyllic beaches and
islands, inlets, shoals and saltings, and the natural beauty of the
surrounding saltmarsh creates a perfect habitat for hundreds of wading
birds. Many of the lonely beaches are too remote for anyone but the

serious hiker, but they can be reached in a small boat, with the added benefit that you can drop anchor and enjoy a swim. The little hamlets and villages that skirt the river's edge provide the cruising sailor with a real glimpse into history, a past that is rich in stories told and retold in the many Inns, pubs and bars. Saltings, filled with a maze of ditches and topped with marshy sea grass, is home to a variety of wading birds and natural flora and fauna. Natural art-like shoal features such as Thirslet Spit, and Mill Point are wonders of natural beauty, for much of the time hidden below the waterline, the geography of which unfolds in a layer of shells on an ebbing tide, and all waiting to be explored by the small-boat sailor. Stretches of the river and some of the creeks are peppered with withies, some marking oyster beds, others marking shallows; slender sticks that can appear eerie and ghostly when the mist gropes its way across the water. These natural features are all places that I have frequented, either in my pocket cruiser, or my little lugsail dinghy.

Essex smack Hyacinth *sailing down river towards the Thirslet buoy.*

I potter for no particular reason other than to enjoy the sheer peace, quiet and solitude, and they are all places any small boat can reach without too much hassle. The River Blackwater is undoubtedly one of the last stretches of water in England still used by many traditional sailing vessels. Smacks, bawleys and iconic sailing barges can be seen regularly, providing the observer with a timeless view into a small chapter of our nation's maritime history. The life of working boat skippers has always been governed by the tides, and this applies in no less degree to today's leisure sailor. If he wants to discover the charms and hidden gems that the river has to offer, and discover the many quiet backwaters, he must learn to use the tides to his advantage. He will then soon realise that in days past, many of these secret places, in quiet corners of inland-jutting creeks and beside working fields, could only be reached by barges and work boats at the top of the tide. Against the backdrop of tanned sails, modern craft and highly-tuned dinghies race against each other on this princely broad estuary, while deep-keeled cruisers appear from creeks that branch off the river, and make their way down to the mouth for a day's sail in the deeper water between the swatchways.

St Peter-on-the-Wall Chapel, sited on the remote Dengie peninsular and overlooking the mouth of the Colne and Blackwater estuaries.

Reminders of different eras can be seen at Bradwell where the power station, built in 1962 and closed eight years ago, overlooks two buildings from a far earlier age: the remote Roman Fort of Othona, built in the 3rd century to deal with the threat posed by the Saxon raiders, and the tiny Chapel of St Peter-on-the-Wall. While hidden in the trees nearby is a solitary cottage, once the home of Walter Linnett, one of the last Blackwater wildfowlers.

The old maritime skills may be dying out, but there are still those endeavouring to preserve them. In a small weather-boarded hut at the top of Woodrolfe Creek, in Tollesbury, a sailmaker continues to work in the traditional way. At the time of writing, he had just made a new sail for *Ardwina*, the Thames sailing barge. Just below Hythe Quay at Maldon there is a small boat yard that continues the work of restoring and maintaining those majestic East Coast work horses.

At Fullbridge, a little further on from Heybridge Creek where the Blackwater becomes the River Chelmer, a shipwright can be found restoring and rebuilding wooden smacks and barges. When I last visited him he was working on the Essex smack *Varuna* and making a new boom for another, the *Excelsior*, with possibly one of the largest pieces of larch to be used around these shores for a number of years.

Thames spritsail barges, a familiar sight on the Blackwater.

Old fishing boats evoke a special charm to this waterside scene at the village green, West Mersea.

Oyster fishing on the Blackwater is a tradition dating back many centuries but it is still being carried out on the river today. Once harvested, oysters are transported around the country but you will not find better than those at the oyster sheds in West Mersea. I have often sat at anchor in my small boat watching the fishermen sifting through the shells by hand, a timeless chore that has not changed for centuries. Concrete pill boxes dot the shore of the river, built to guard against the threat of invasion by enemy aircraft. Osea Island was used as a naval base for torpedo boats and behind Bradwell power station lies the remains of Bradwell Bay airfield, a busy fighter base during the war, from which many of Britain's cross-Channel missions were launched. Some creeks have become the final resting place for tired sailing barges, such as *Snowdrop*, whose skeleton can still be seen in Goldhanger Creek, and *Unity* in Sampson's Creek. Old hulks also lay in the saltings. The wrecks of the *Memory* and the Yarmouth boat, *Pilot Jack*, can be seen part buried in the Tollesbury mud.

Amid the lunar-like scenery of the mudflats birds feed on gently sloping mud. Grassy mounds are lined with an array of colourful flowers and plants, such as sea lavender, samphire and marigold. Seals can often be seen sunbathing in the mud and swimming in the river, while the chattering of bird life seems almost constant, especially when the tide is out. Due to the huge area of saltmarsh and tidal reaction, the river is well-known for being one of the saltiest in the country. Ancient communities once gathered salt from the river and this salt-making tradition continues at Maldon where salt crystals are gathered just as they would have been years earlier.

The Blackwater is a river of many secret havens, providing peaceful watery retreats from the rigours of modern life. The river is also a small-boat sailor's treasure trove, with scores of delightful places to visit and explore, all satisfying and rewarding. Whether you seek the solitude of a peaceful anchorage or a more intrusive village community life, there is plenty of sailing adventure in and about the Blackwater that awaits the pocket or dinghy cruiser.

*"This week the Blackwater creeks would
be full to the brim at high water"*

Chapter Two
Across The Stumble

THE excitement had been building steadily as the day went on. I tried to concentrate but my thoughts kept drifting to images of the little pocket cruising yacht *Huffler* crawling gently along the lonely muddy bank of Ford Creek. Spare time at work the previous week had been spent planning a visit to this creek. The name Ford stands for a shallow place for crossing a river on foot, which is appropriate as it sits beside the Roman built Osea causeway.

Although its entrance is just over a mile in distance from my mooring at Goldhanger, the whole area dries out around here, at which time the creek is hidden from view by the mudflats of The Stumble.

*An ancient wooden
structure, preserved by
the deep Stumble mud.*

The Stumble itself is one of the most important Neolithic sites in the east of England. Its deep mud is thought to contain signs of ancient human life from as far back as 4000BC. Although no longer visible, there was an island of saltmarsh called the Wild Hills, which remained visible at high water up until the 1950s.

Today the shallowest area can be found where a yellow race can marked WH is placed each summer by Goldhanger Sailing Club. Creeks such as Goldhanger, Ford, Earl and Stumble Drain carve their way through all this silvery mud that covers the ground from my mooring to the island of Osea. In the 1940s these creeks of the upper river would have been a haunt of wildfowlers, who would use punts to gain access to the mass of wading birds that feed off the rich grounds at low water, and who today are joined by the wintering brent geese that visit the area in their thousands. I like to visit these creeks to enjoy the spectacular wildlife and soak up the special atmosphere. For the ditch-crawler, Ford Creek presents its own problem. To appreciate its muddy banks fully it has to be entered from the south side of the river around low water.

Full sail... heading across The Stumble from Goldhanger.

I could be there near high water with my anchor set in a mere 15 minutes as this creek sits directly across the causeway. But then that would mean a long wait of four to five hours until the tide had retreated enough for me to play among its muddy banks. I prefer to make this trip a bit more fun by visiting one or two creeks on the southern shore first, before returning across The Stumble and circumnavigating Osea Island, which means arriving at the entrance to Ford Creek at just about the right time. I was able to get away early, on the way grabbing a few tins of food and some milk to last for a two-day cruise. High water was at 1506 hrs, so the fact that I arrived at my mooring with six minutes to spare was cutting it fine, to say the least. "Damn it," I muttered to myself. "I have to get over to Southey Creek pretty quickly because it dries out about two hours after high water." The forecast was unsettled, a strong westerly threatening thunder storms and showers.

Raising the yard, I thought of reefing the mainsail. But, not wanting to interrupt momentum by stopping any longer, I cleated the halyards and cast off. *Huffler* came alive immediately as the staysail rolled out, followed by the jib. The tides around this time were perfect for my destined creek, bumper springs of over 6 metres. This week the Blackwater creeks would be full to the brim at high water. More importantly, the banks of Ford Creek would be fully revealed and navigable around the low water mark.

It was now 1536 hrs. The wind thrashed at *Huffler's* sails, forcing me to take hold of her grabrail as she lunged forward, thirstily reaching into the main river. The course was set for Southey Creek. We quickly passed the North Double buoy where a squall that swept down the river sent *Huffler* reeling on her ear and gave me a good soaking. A few minutes later we romped passed the No 4 Southey buoy. On reaching the shallow water of Southey Creek, and abreast of Northey Island, we readied-about for Limbourne Creek which, thankfully, was still full of water, and was to be our berth for the night. On entering the saltmarsh-lined creek and crawling along the east bank, I was struck by the profusion of purple sea lavender. At this stage I decided to ease *Huffler's* main until we were only just moving enough for steerage.

Sailing this slowly enabled me to savour the delights of this lovely little creek. Limbourne has a depth of 3-5 feet and, apart from a couple of stumps at its head, is a safe place to anchor. I finally chose to run the boat to a stop in the mud at the top and dropped the hook over the starboard side. Pleased with the first part of this two-day creek crawl, I spent a peaceful night watching the stars appear, *Huffler* sitting cheerfully on the mud before I chose to turn in.

Limbourne Creek, a peaceful anchorage.

The following morning called for an early rise as high water was at 0327 hrs. I reckoned on leaving the creek with enough water to return via Southey at 0430 hrs, which worked well.

A new dawn was swiftly upon us, along with wonderful shades of pink, mixed with tinges of orange, covering the big eastern sky.

I sailed out of Southey Creek and continued north to Osea Island's old Roman causeway where there is a good 8 feet of water at high tide. The westerly wind combined with the ebb to provide an exhilarating sail. I had the whole tide to play on. The golden sand of Shipwreck Beach was a mere 30-40 feet away on my starboard side and I had stopped here many times this season for a picnic or a swim in its clear waters. A magical place. There is enough water to cruise along this shoreline above Earl Creek two hours either side of high water. This is also a good place to dry out for the night as the mud is quite even all the way along, and slopes very gently away from the island. At high water, from the northern side of Osea Island, a small boat can find its way into a magnificent golden cove of shingle and sand at the most easterly point. On a sunny day with blue skies above, Osea resembles almost a South Pacific island, a scene that will leave a lasting impression on any visitor. Rounding the point I could see cormorants on the shingly top waiting for a seafood breakfast.

The enigmatic Osea Island, an Essex jewel.

Nearing Marconi Sailing Club's moorings, it was now 0545 hrs. Rounding *Huffler* again, this time into the fast ebbing waters of the narrows. It was obviously going to be a hard beat against the westerly wind and spring ebb. But a good challenge, too. An hour later, and still beating past the pill boxes on Osea, we reached the shallow water of The Bay by Stansgate Abbey and Steeple Creek, but it was not until we were passed Lawling Creek and Cooper's Creek that the tide began to ease. Much of the ground gained on one tack was immediately lost on the next, but it was great fun on this beautiful morning. I had managed to brew a cuppa beside the emerging mudflats of the Doctor, where a large survey vessel lay at anchor menacingly towering over the little *Huff*. Here the stretch of beach reaches towards West Point and is a delight for naturalists. A small boat can safely anchor about 50 feet from the shingle shoreline to dry out on soft sand. For many sailors who pass along its shores, the fact that Osea is a private island adds to its enigma. Since the Romans built the causeway across from the mainland to its 400 acres of arable farmland it has had many owners. Even William the Conqueror's nephew once owned the island, as did the Earl of Essex. In 1900 the 10-bedroom Edwardian-style manor house was built on its southern shore and in 1903 Frederick Charrington, the brewer, became the owner turning it into a centre for temperance.

The Charringtons had a steamboat called *Annie* rebuilt at Cook's Yard, Maldon, and ran day trips from the promenade down to Osea pier.

Osea pier. A local landmark used by some to gauge the depth of water, but built in the early 1900s to enable the Steamship Annie *to land day-trippers from Maldon.*

Just east of the pier is perhaps one of the prettiest of little creeks, Oak Tree Creek. At high tide the sea gently cuts through the shingle into an area of saltmarsh which has beautiful oak trees overhanging the creek. This creates a unique 'secret garden' atmosphere which can be experienced in a small dinghy. The forces took over the island during WW1 when it was used as a naval base housing torpedo boats up to 75 feet in length, as well as various other officer and staff buildings. These fast and agile boats were sent on missions to places like Zebrugge and Ostend in Belgium. A concrete slipway with tracks used to launch these boats is still visible east of the pier. In recent years the tranquil island has been a retreat centre attracting some high-profile celebrities. The island is presently a quiet resort offering accommodation for weekend or week-long stays in the manor house or farm cottages.

Torpedo boat launch tracks, still visible east of Osea pier.

After a night sail up from Old Mill Creek in October 2010 I awoke the following morning to a commotion going on across the mudflats at Osea. I have never seen so many people in this area, and doubt I ever will again. Harry Potter star Daniel Radcliffe and a crew of around 80 were on the causeway at low water filming The Woman In Black, a ghost tale.

River trips down to Osea can still be booked on the *Viking Saga* from the promenade at Maldon, and there is a small ferry service from Heybridge that regularly visits the island.

I reached the Southey Creek buoy again 20 minutes before low water, by which time it was beginning to lean over. I tacked in 3 foot of water between here and the North and South Double port and starboard buoys. The latter, was sitting high on the mud. *Huffler's* plate now becoming audible on every tack. Not a single boat dared venture out at this state of the tide and my little ship had full reign of the muddy kingdom. The fruits of my labour were almost ripe as the climax of this two-day creek crawl approached on my starboard side, the elusive Ford Creek. No salt marsh-fringed banks line this creek, just pure Essex mud of the deepest variety, and an abundance of birdlife, most of which were gulls. The noise from the birds was incredible. They lined the muddy brows as if on parade for this rarest of visitor, the cruising yachtsman.

Elated that everything had worked out as planned, I guided *Huffler* to the steadiness of the mud where I furled her sails. Although close to the middle of the upper river, this creek is a sanctuary of solitude for roughly five hours of a spring tide when it again hides itself beneath the murky waters. With the new flood freeing *Huffler* from the mud I unfurled both the staysail and jib and crept into the creek. With just 1-2 foot of water beneath me I began using the sounding-pole, gliding silently among the wildlife and following in the footsteps of the old Blackwater wildfowlers who would have used this small creek in their shallow punts. Although they would have been looking for a meal, I have brought mine along with me, dropping anchor in 3 feet of water between the west of Osea Island and Decoy Point for a well-earned breakfast of eggs and bacon.

Another bonus of visiting at this state of tide is Larnch Creek, which can be seen twisting through the mud before it passes under the Osea causeway. Even further up there are two small wrecks at Decoy Saltings and if drying out near the seawall, it is easy to get ashore and enjoy stunning views back across the mudflats.

Just after breakfast the sun came out from between the clouds casting a huge rainbow across the river and three hours later the whole creek, along with the birdlife had vanished from view. The river was now alive again as another huge thunder squall passed over giving a mighty shake.

A brisk end to two days of wonderful cruising on the Blackwater.

Ford Creek revealed. The low water creek curves around Osea's West Point.

Looking south at low water from Decoy Creek. The two small wrecks are clearly visible. This area is navigable for two hours around high water and is an interesting place to dry out. The entrance to Ford Creek can be seen to the left in the distance off the main river.

*"My thoughts of those smugglers of old evoke
images of quiet moonlight passages "*

Chapter Three
Smugglers and Jupiter

HIGH TAXES placed on certain goods such as alcohol during the 18th
and early 19th centuries gave rise to smuggling of contraband in and
about the river. At this time smugglers mingled amongst the daily goings
on of the fishermen and bargemen. With the sheer volume of smuggling
going on among the myriad of creeks and shallow waters the revenue
cutters had their hands full. During this time the chapel of St Peter-on-
the-Wall on the outskirts of Bradwell, situated as it is on such a remote
shore was occasionally used for the storing of contraband. Smugglers
landing on or sailing across the remote and shallow mudflats would have
been out of reach of the deeper keels of the revenue boats. My thoughts
of those smugglers of old evoke images of quiet moonlight passages,
made with the sounds of the sea lapping at the water's edge, or the
muffled sound of an oar in its rowlock as the smugglers boat nears the
creek or inlets head before scraping her keel on the shore. Although I
prefer this romantic vision, author Hervey Benham tells of more sobering
tales portraying the harsh reality of the violent conflict between the
smugglers and the revenue men. I had decided to make my own
moonlight passage in the footsteps of those smugglers. The weather in the
previous month of August was very unsettled, and with plenty of rain,
combined with strong winds, it hampered many of my attempts to get
afloat. The latest forecast in late September of three days sunshine and

temperatures reaching 22 degrees was very encouraging. With spring tides due there would also be a full moon. Not only would the moon be shining brightly but right beside it the planet Jupiter would be shining, too. Coincidently but very conveniently for me, astronomers had

From Weymarks to Sales Point beach, natural Essex beauty.

predicted Jupiter would be the brightest it has ever been for two thousand years. The two natural forms of light combined would be a torchlight painted on the sea's surface … Just what I needed to make the passage. As long as the sky was clear of clouds, it would be possible to guide *Huffler's* inquisitive bow out to the extremes of the river mouth and south, over the shallow mudflats of St Peter's. This would also be my first venture alone at night under sail.

I began the cruise like dozens I had made earlier in the year, from my mud mooring at Goldhanger Creek. High water was at 1206 hrs with low water at 1738 hrs. Like other north shore creeks, Goldhanger was an ideal place for smugglers to creep into under cover of darkness, when a horse and cart would have quickly been on its way up the lanes to Tiptree Heath, a place where smuggled goods were taken before being moved to London and elsewhere. The local pub, The Chequers, is reputed to have been used to store contraband in its cellar. Even today the creek has some nice shingle stretches of shoreline where you can run a boat up.

Inside Bawley Creek facing east. One story I have heard about this creek is that its name derives from a man who once lived here on board a bawley, (a wooden fishing boat similar to a smack). The small opening in the saltings to the left of the farm wharf ahead is Death Creek, which exits east of Osea Island.

I raised the mains'l and sailed out of the creek heading south, crossing Stumble Drain and Earl Creek before creeping through the saltmarsh at Osea Island and into Bawley Creek. The entrance is just under a mile across the river from Goldhanger and is easily found during the warmer months as a race can is placed near to it marked DM. There is a small wharf in here where farm barges once loaded. From the wharf Death Creek winds eastward inside the saltmarsh. This shallow tiny creek starts in the mudflats a little further east from Osea Island's East Point where it is not navigable. The navigable stretch of creek can be found by entering the saltings at the pill box where there is just a few feet at high water neaps. Quite a bit of erosion is taking place here and the creek has lost quite a large section of its saltmarsh bank. If entering Bawley Creek from the dock end there are a couple locally placed white transit markers pointing out the deeper water. When you are sailing in a mere few feet the deeper water means a few more inches, which is very useful. There are rumours as to how the name Death Creek came about. It is thought that back in the days when smugglers went about their business under cover of darkness, a boat was found swinging on its anchor full of men with their throats cut. This seems to be a very reasonable rumour, but one that can be found associated with other creeks also. Despite this gruesome tale Death Creek is a delightful little creek, with stunning views down river to the open sea, giving it its own special atmosphere. It is well worth a visit near the top of a spring tide. Like Goldhanger, this creek comes alive with migratory birds in the winter. They gather in such large numbers that the noise levels reach incredible decibels, making a sound that resembles a pack of barking dogs. The creek is extremely shallow in places, especially at its eastern end where it is difficult to find water through the mudflats, but from Bawley Creek between 2-5 foot of water can be found all the way through Death Creek to East Point. As I sailed *Huffler* through here under tiny staysail the paddle was in constant use. Being late September the creek's gin-clear water allowed a good view of the muddy sea bed beneath. I could not resist sailing its saltmarsh-lined length twice. Beside the wharf are a few finger inlets with many old stumps showing signs of bygone activity. By the time I exited out of the shallower eastern end, the tide had begun its ebb. The winds being light I had planned on help from the tide, the boat drifted slowly down river, passing Collin's Creek buoy where at low water an ancient tidal fish trap can be seen. I lay becalmed here until *Huffler* was pulled south into the deeper water of the main river channel where the spring tide's force pulled us along eastward.

Three hours later I gently put the anchor down in two feet of water beside Pewet Island, another of the river's ancient fish traps. The trap is made up of hundreds of eroded wooden stumps over a thousand years old. The stumps reach out into the river north eastward to the low water line. I sat and observed the stumps that disappeared into the shallow water. Still hoping more wind would begin blowing. And it did, up come the anchor followed by the sails and within minutes *Huffler* was turning to starboard at the tide pole and beating her way into Bradwell Creek.

A well preserved ancient fish trap dating from the 5ᵗʰ century AD stretches out into the river from Pewet Island.

Meandering along the beautiful Death Creek.

Huffler's full sails setting nicely to the rising southerly wind, enabling her to make over the ebb and I sailed deep into the creek, passed the marina and then circled through the moored yachts before running here into the mud beside the twisted poles of the former barge quay. The poles originally extended high above to fend off moored barges in the event of extreme weather during high spring tides that threatened to wash them up onto the quay. Up until 1932 a local farming family of barge owners, the Parkers, had 26 barges working from here. If they ever did come in this small creek at the same time it would have been an impressive sight.

A mooring buoy sat 5 feet away in the mud so I wouldn't need to drop anchor. After putting the sea-boots on I tied the boat to it and then clambered over 30 feet of sloping mud to the saltmarsh bank. Small rills in the bank were home to a couple of perishing clinker skiffs, inside them rusted metal engine blocks still stood up giving the impression they just could have some life left in them.

Bradwell Quay. The twisted poles of the former barge wharf still remain. Behind the quay to the east is Down Hall beach.

I got onto the seawall at Down Hall and had a look back along the creek at *Huffler*. With the hastily retreating tide she was now sitting high on the mud. I had a pleasant walk past the now decommissioned nuclear power station. Immediately in front of it at the water's edge is a golden beach that could be from a Caribbean setting.

Haystacks piled high along the former Bradwell Bay airfield.

Bradwell Creek, view looking west. A seemingly large number of moored yachts·fill the creek, which makes sailing through here interesting. A truly charming creek to spend a quiet evening after an active day's sailing.

On the fields nearby was the disused runway of Bradwell Bay airfield. The runway was now being used to store the summer wheat harvest from the surrounding fields. Huge house-sized stacks were placed along its length. It would have been this kind of cargo that kept the Parker fleet busy during the age of sail. The stretch of beach past the power station to the outfall pipe at Weymarks is littered with wooden stumps that are a hazard at anything other than high water, but after the pipe and to the Sales Point lighters prospects for a safe landing are improved. This stretch of beach is one of the most beautiful beaches in Essex and at high tide the two small creeks that cut into Weymarks and Sales Point saltings can be navigated in a dinghy. Time was moving on so I made my way back along the seawall. I just had enough time for a jar in the Green Man where I contemplated the coming moonlight passage before getting back to the boat.

Sales Point Creek sits hidden behind the golden shoreline of the main river. The creek is perhaps one of the more difficult small creeks to get into due to its remote location, but it is still worth the effort.

In the deep mud I try to retrace footsteps with the hope that if I got there safely I will be able to return. Well, that's the theory . . . about ten feet from the boat I sank to my waste causing me to scramble forward desperately and, suddenly I took the form of an Olympic diver as I slid forward flat out, grasping at the buoy's ground chain. Pulling myself up I clambered aboard in a sorry state, completely covered in mud. With not a sole around this could well have been my final mud berth, just like the nearby wrecks and withering old dock posts. Wasting the next valuable hour cleaning the mud away the returning flood water had reached *Huffler's* stern and darkness was upon us. How glad I was it had become dark! Mud covered everything, so I gave up trying to sponge it off and, instead, put on some clean clothes and had something to eat. All the while I kept an eye watching the full moon and Jupiter's glow, looking for any signs of a mist or cloud that might mask the night light for the intended passage. The moment had come. With everything set I pulled out *Huffler's* staysail and fired up her small outboard. The time was now 2210 hrs so, letting go the mooring line, we glided forward. We all have a unique way of dealing with stresses that we place upon our minds and bodies; the senses become heightened as if in tune with everything around us, enabling complete focus on the job in hand.

The southerly wind was blowing nicely, about a force 3 as *Huffler* wriggled her way between the moored boats under moonlight. Passing close to the Starboard buoy silhouette then heading towards the flashing light of the tide pole. As we reached the mouth of the creek I was able to raise *Huffler's* mainsail and cut the engine. The sail from here to Sales Point was truly magical and I savoured every moment.

Sales Point barge lighters act as a wavebreak to protect the fragile shoreline. For small-boat sailors they provide a good bearing when crossing over St Peter's mudflats into Gunner's Creek or the Ray Sand Channel.

The lights on Mersea and Tollesbury were twinkling. Out to sea the flashing lights of the Bench Head and North West Knoll buoys were reliably guiding seafarers who might fancy a moonlight passage. Making just two knots against the flood I had allowed two hours for the passage and by 2300 hrs the drain pipe at Sales Point was abeam to starboard. It took a while for the red lights of the Sales Point lighters to come into view but when they did so did the swells. The closer I got to the open sea the higher the waves became. With my local knowledge of the seabed here I kept close to the steel barge lighters, feeling my way around onto the shallow mudflats. There was a slight east to the southerly wind, which created breaking waves over the lighters and on the eastern shore of the Dengie. The large swells created a mesmerizing pattern of moonlight as it reflected off them, and one could only think of those smugglers of old in their boats as they made way into the shore laden with contraband. *Huffler* began rising and pitching to the larger swells as we now headed south, and we had to beat out to sea and back to maintain a southerly course from the last lighter. The sound of the sea was now as crisp as ever. Just as ancient mariners a thousand years or more ago would have done, I made out the dark silhouette of St Peter-on-the-Wall Chapel. The area of mudflats from the barge lighters to the chapel are littered with obstructions which are a danger to any boat. I had allowed for these hazards by keeping a bearing from the last lighter until past the chapel where it was safe to the head in westward on a reach. Although thankful for the glow provided by the moon and Jupiter, it was still dangerously dark with wave upon wave breaking over the approaching saltmarsh. Surrounded by breaking waves in 3 feet of water, it seemed to take a while to find the entrance to Gunner's Creek. When I finally did I quickly downed the main and continued deeper in under staysail. Gaining comfort in the lee of the saltmarsh, *Huffler's* plate began singing loudly but, thinking ahead, I just managed to about-turn, which enabled us to drift astern into the 8 foot wide creek. Raising the plate fully, I used the paddle to guide my little boat deeper into the narrows of the creek, and towards the chapel. Furling the staysail, I went forward and dropped the anchor at 2350 hrs, the funnelling force of the tide giving a nice bite.

Sitting comfortably in Gunner's Creek. The slice in the mud a pleasant reminder of the night before.

Reaching the tiny Gunner's Creek also meant I had visited every creek in the Blackwater estuary from here to the Chelmer river at Fullbridge, its very top. Gunner's Creek is one of numerous inlets and outfalls that indent this remote eastern shore of the Dengie. Not long after anchoring in the comfort and safety below the chapel, a thick mist came over from the south completely obscuring any vision. How glad I was that I had made it safely into the creek! The whole atmosphere was eerie. If I had brought along some barrels of spirit it would have been an easy task to run across the saltmarsh to hide them in the chapel, unseen and unheard by a single soul. At 0200 hrs *Huffler* was sitting comfortably on the creek bed where a sound night's sleep was had. When I arose early the next morning mist still covered the air, but the pleasing sight of the chapel could be made out, as could the small black weather-boarded cottage, the former home to one of the Blackwater's last professional wildfowlers Walter Linnett, who lived a solitary and self-sufficient life so close to nature in this quiet and remote corner of Essex. The cottage is now used by bird watchers as the saltings it overlooks are part of a nature reserve and habitat for many visiting sea birds. After breakfast an enjoyable time was spent here investigating the chapel and cottage, also taking in with every breath of fresh sea air the wonderment of the mystery and solitude of the wide mudflats. The chapel was built in 654AD by St Cedd on the 12 feet thick walls of the Roman fort Othona, hence its name. Half of the fort has been lost to the sea where there would have been a quay for visiting ships to come alongside. The chapel is not only a significant landmark for mariners, but it is thought to be the oldest church still standing in England. I also spent an hour winkle picking on the mudflats, every once in a while a huge explosion from the Shoeburyness firing range shaking the peaceful air. It would be high water at 1300 hrs today which would enable me to sail out of the creek at 1130 hrs to take the flood tide back up to my mooring. Thanks to smugglers and Jupiter this had been a magnificent late September cruise.

Looking across the saltmarsh. St Peter-on-the-Wall Chapel is a prominent feature (centre), with Linnett's cottage to the left surrounded by trees, and a bird-watcher's tower on the right.

"Huffler was conceived for this shallow and muddy environment"

Chapter Four
Wild and Wonderful Saltings

BE IT the dinghy-friendly marsh creek at Weymarks' beach or the lumpy tufts of grass that crown the muddy islands in Wilkin's Creek, wild and wonderful saltings proliferate the fringes of the Blackwater estuary. The rising tides cover much of the land in low-lying areas and, because the sea water leaves accumulating salty deposits as it retreats, these areas become habitable only by salt-tolerant plant life, on which other hardy grasses are able to grow. This continual process of inter-tidal action creates the saltmarsh, or 'saltings', as they are known. There is an added marvel to these glorious marshes in that they are a natural defence barrier against the ravages of the sea, acting like a sponge, by soaking up the overflowing spring tides. There are a few larger areas I have found of particular interest as a small-boat sailor, such as Tollesbury Saltings, Old Hall Marshes, and Salcott. An active day's sailing can be had around all these saltings, and part of the fun exploring them is experiencing the sudden variations in the depth of water, which adds to the excitement. In a light boat, the adventurous sailor should be able to push off into deep water again with a paddle or oar if he grounds. I usually enjoy sailing around the saltings alone, but I like to take my children along for a 'top-of-the-tide' sail. They get great pleasure from simply drifting about in the maze of ditches and islands created at high water and manoeuvring the boat through tiny bends and alleys while brushing the top sides against the green and fawn coloured grasses. Thrift, sea lavender and sea aster paint many of these areas with a pleasing purple glow across the sea grass in the warm days around July. It was one July day that I steered *Huffler* out of the charming Big Fleet Creek into the main river, and slipped the boat across the nearby Shinglehead Point heading for Old Hall Creek. The two channels here are known locally as the 'Leavings', a name first adopted by fishermen who would regularly leave their boats here. As I headed inland, a glance at my watch showed it was a couple of hours to high tide. The light southerly winds were just perfect for exploring the small creeks and rills that cut deep into the marshes and the boat moved gently along, passing Little and Great Cob Islands before turning west

Big Fleet Creek can be found just above Shinglehead Point, on the river's north shore. Before the seawall dam was built the waterway was a major tidal fleet cutting through Tollesbury Wick natural marshland.

into Woodrolfe Creek and the depths of the marsh that spread all around like a soft carpet. The Tollesbury Wick Marshes, from Mell Creek to the Marina, cover 600 acres of nature reserve and are managed by the Essex Wildlife Trust. They are a classic example of natural marsh, having never been ploughed. Woodrolfe Hard was only a short distance ahead, but time allowed a push on the tiller for a short visit into Curlew Creek to glimpse the hulk of *Saltcote Belle* and the remains of a torpedo boat, both which have become home to a number of ducks. *Huffler* was conceived for this shallow and muddy environment but I too was in my element. I pushed the boom over while hardening her cleated staysail and she quietly glided back into Woodrolfe Creek. This took us into the Back Creek where there are mud moorings all down one side. These charming berths all have their own individual pontoons, which are interlinked with rustic wooden planked walkways. And here there is also another ageing hulk, the sailing barge *Memory*, which sits snugly in a ditch that cuts off the creek. You can get right up beside her in a small boat, and her name is still clearly discernible on her broad transom.

The hulk of Thames sailing barge Memory *slowly decaying on the saltings. Images like this are still a common sight along our rivers and creeks of the Thames Estuary.*

Circling around, I sailed back into Woodrolfe, or 'Woodup' Creek, as it is often called. The unmissable bright red Trinity lightship was passed to starboard. She is home to FACT, the Fellowship Afloat Charitable Trust which runs adventure activity courses for young people. The Trust once used the *Memory* as its base. Sadly her interior was destroyed by a fire in 1990. The Trust owns 147 acres of saltings on this side of the creek and I can't think of a better environment in which to introduce youngsters to sailing. At the end of the creek the 150-year-old Grade 2 listed Granary shed somehow still stands erect on the hard. High spring tides now wash these old timbers regularly with sea water. Over the years the shed has been used for a variety of roles, including storage associated with the barge and fishing trades, as well as boatbuilding. The shed was a finalist in the 2006 BBC TV programme called Restoration Village. Tollesbury Sailing Club members launch their dinghies from the hard here and on the highest of spring tides it is even possible to 'street sail' up the middle of the road past the boat yard and up to the cream-painted yacht stores.

Woodrolfe Hard and Granary shed viewed from Bontin's Creek. The shoal draft cruiser can reach the hard up to three hours either side of high water.

This stretch of water from the hard is known locally as Bontin's Creek where today there was enough water to sail in front of the salt water bathing pool. Once a remote fishing village, Tollesbury has become home to many cruising yachts based in the marina. There is also a useful chandlery and other associated services nearby. After a spell on the marshes in peaceful surroundings it is nice to take a look at civilisation again, and a walk up to the Tollesbury Light House tearoom for a cuppa is not a bad way to do it; or, perhaps, a visit to St Mary's Church, which has a colourful 'Seafarers Window'. The stained glass window was a gift from an American in the 1960s to mark Tollesbury's links with the sea. The window depicts some of the early America's Cup yachts on which noted Tollesmen sailed during the months when their fishing smacks were laid up in the creeks.

The window also contains working boats that sailed the Essex coast, a smack under sail and a 'stackie' barge. The enchantment of days gone by grips me whenever I come to Tollesbury, the village of the plough and sail. I seem to end up dreaming of ways to obtain a houseboat and live here. For such a small area, so many creeks shoot off enticingly in all directions giving the creek-crawler a feeling of being a child in a sweetshop. Leaving Woodrolfe Creek *Huffler* floated over a clump of mud called the 'Whale' and

The writing at the bottom of the window reads "Follow Me And I Will Make You Fishers Of Men"

headed west into Bowles Creek, which is to port of Brand's saltings, the island of saltmarsh ahead. The central island of marsh is owned by Tollesbury Wildfowlers. I thought it best not to go up as far as Horseshoe Creek, that tiny dog-leg bend, as I needed to get back over the flood. I spun the little ship round in the mouth of Johnny's Creek, another small but beautiful waterway and returned through Chatterson's Creek. This lovely stretch of water was once the oyster layings to the Chatterson family. During the early 20th century many oyster fishermen were based in Tollesbury, and in its hey-day up to 80 smacks would have lined the creeks right up to the hard.

But time was moving on, and with about three quarters of an hour of flood left I crept into Old Hall Creek.

Bowles Creek, facing south. Chatterson's Creek can be found in the saltings to the right of this image. Old Hall Creek heads north between the mud bank and saltmarsh to the left.
Many wooden stumps can be found along the shoreline here. The level mud gives a sound night's sleep if drying out.

The cream-painted yacht stores at Tollesbury were built around 1900. Set on stilts with external step ladders pointing up to pitched roofs, these quaint little wooden buildings served the many high-class yachts that would often come up the creek at the time, as well as the local fishing fleet.

I adore these saltings so much that I had planned for today's cruise to culminate deep in the marsh by high water so that I could spend a night under the golf ball size stars, far away from any form of man-made noise or distraction. It is only then that the sweet chirping melodies can be heard from the grey plover, redshank and curlew. Now in Old Hall Creek, I had reached Drake's Hard, an outlying former wharf. This was a busy boat repairers' hard in the early 1900s. Smacks, barges and coasters would bring up here. Served by a small community that had its own pub, the Ship Ahoy Inn, which, apart from serving ship sailors with ale, has links to smuggling in the 18th century. The posts of the wharf are still in a recognisable condition, with bits of old dock line strung from timbers that look as if they have been there for centuries.

Old Hall Creek, The former Ship Ahoy Inn ahead.

The hard continued to be used by barges up until the 1950s. The pub was in a small row of cottages that are still here. The saltings here were purchased in 1984 by the RSPB and are now part of Old Hall Marshes nature reserve. Past the wharf I furled the sails and reached for the paddle to continue under 'oar and tide'. This next reach of creek is a marshman's delight as you are now absorbed by the beauty of this wilderness. With gentle propulsion from the odd paddle stroke, *Huffler* rounded a succession of sharp turns in the creek, whose depth was now down to a mere three feet and its width twice that of the boat. The final 100 feet or so of creek terminated at the 'cant' which was draped in places by the edible leaves of sea purslane. Here the now stream-like water began circling around the boat, bubbles swirled into a vortex created by paddle and hull against the sea water's slow but unstinting movement. The tide lines were now brimming in full glory. Silver ripples shimmered in the reflection of the afternoon sun; cattle grazed across the rugged grassland; butterflies hovered over the marsh; and huge dragonflies came and went.

The weathered timbers at Drake's Hard hint at a once busy creek.

Beneath the wide, open sky above, flocks of birds flew by painting patterns with their synchronised movements. I had taken my seat for the evening's sunset by laying *Huffler* just off the 'cant' grass and setting her anchor. It was time to cook a meal and ready the bunk below . . . Ah, the joys of the saltings!

Many of the creeks contain an area of saltings that can be navigated. Most of these saltings abut a seawall that, like the majority in Essex, were built during the 17th to 19th centuries so as the enclosed land could be used for agriculture or building purposes. Over the years some areas of the river have experienced erosion, resulting in a loss of natural saltmarsh

Close quarter work; using the paddle to explore the saltings at the top of Old Hall Creek.

habitat for wildlife. As a counter-measure to the effects of this erosion there is a coastal realignment project in operation inside the river.

The sites are at Northey Island, Orplands near Bradwell, Tollesbury, and Abbots Hall. At these sites a stretch of seawall has been breached to allow tidal waters into the natural levels. Over time this re-establishes the natural coastal habitat such as the saltmarsh. The Abbots Hall site became the largest in Europe to be realigned when Essex Wildlife Trust, which owns the site, breached 3.5 km of seawall there in 2002. The breach created over 200 acres of inter-tidal saltmarsh that has become home to an impressive array of resident and wintering birds.

Abbotts Hall Creek also has a farm wharf and the historic Ship Lock as well as many red hills. The area is thought to have been a landing place since Roman times. As part of the project the dock was completely refurbished in 2001 making it possible for Thames barges to dock here once more.

Abbots Hall Creek has its own farm wharf called The Ship Lock where produce could be stored protected from high tides, before being loaded onto a barge and taken to London.
In May 2011 and as a celebration of her rebuild, the Thames barge Dawn made a nostalgic sail down to London after loading hay from the wharf.

Further up Salcott Creek there is a delightful small area teaming with tiny ditches around 6 feet wide. I down the sails and enjoy poling about in here. If staying the night, the mud is comfortably flat and you can get up on the seawall for a walk into the village.

Even near low tide there is some water in Little Ditch. The creek takes you into Copt Hall Saltings.

Little Ditch is also a good place to reach inland through the saltmarsh. The name can be deceiving. Yes it is small but in reality it is actually a very deep creek. Generally the saltings are accessible from around two hours before high water but Little Ditch, also known as Copt Hall Creek is an exception, having some water four hours after high tide. I have had some beautiful moments sailing here, zig-zagging to the very top of the creek where red hills can be seen from the seawall. The delightful picture-perfect little church of St Nicholas can also be seen and is an easy walk. Inside the church an old newspaper headline hangs framed on the wall. It tells the story of how the peace and quiet of this small hamlet of Little Wigborough was shattered at two o'clock one eventful morning in 1916 by the crash-landing of a huge 620 foot German enemy Zeppelin airship. It had just bombed London and was trying to return across the Channel when it was hit by anti-aircraft fire. After crashing beside the church at Copt Hall the Germans set light to their gigantic machine before walking off down the road towards Peldon where they were eventually picked up by local police.

The Blackwater estuary is a designated Site of Special Scientific Interest (SSSI) so hopefully these saltings, along with much of the river and its creeks, will be preserved unspoilt for future generations to enjoy.

Plough meets sail. Huffler *sits snug in a narrow cut, while a farmer ploughs the fields bounding* Salcott Creek.

"A mass of ropes strung fore and aft,
way up high to the topmasts"

Chapter Five
To Maldon

Maldon, a haven for traditional craft. Barges Reminder, Hydrogen *and* Kitty *among others can be chartered from the Hythe by day-trippers. The Sailing Barge Trust moors* Pudge *and* Centuar *here, and offers opportunities for those wanting to learn how to sail and maintain these stately craft.*

VISITING the salty town of Maldon makes a refreshing change after spending time in the wilderness of the outlying creeks. As you round Herring Point, ahead of you in the distant landscape is the town's most prominent feature, the steeple-capped church tower of St Mary, 'the fishermen's church'. It nestles beside barge masts topped with colourful bobs that flap proudly in the breeze. The tower has been a beacon to shipping for generations, its view softened by treetops rising from the Edwardian promenade. It is a pretty picture that has not changed much over the centuries. Approaching Maldon waterfront is like stepping back in time, to an age when sail ruled the waves on this river. A large number of restored Thames sailing barges dominate the quayside here and provide the visitor with a living museum of working sail. Maldon was once home to many stack barges. The 'stackie', as they were known, could be distinguished by the short staysail set high up the forestay, along with a reefed mainsail hanging from a long sprit. This rig enabled the sails to be set over the bales of straw or hay that towered above the decks. The skipper at the helm had limited visibility so the mate would often sit up on the hay stacks and shout directions down to the skipper.

The stack barge would mainly fetch hay to London for the horses, and return with their muck to be used as fertiliser on local fields. Other typical barge cargoes included timber, grain, corn, cement, chalk, stone, coal and even beer. In the late 19th and early 20th centuries there were many yards building barges along the East Coast, two of the main ones at Maldon being John Howard, who built the majority of barges here and Walter Cook & Son, each easily distinguished by their own style of craftsmanship. Stack barges were flat-bottomed and wide, almost like a large oblong box. This shape enabled economic transportation of large amounts of cargo, while the shallow draft would allow a skipper and mate access to small farm wharfs or mills that were situated among the myriad of tiny creeks that indent the Thames Estuary.

Not only could a stackie take a big load of bulky cargo, but it also meant the barge could sit flat on the mud without toppling. It is a testament to their skills that the yards were able to produce barges with aesthetically pleasing lines and pretty curves.

Maldon was once a very busy fishing port where old hands used traditional methods right up to the 1960s and 70s, so it is no wonder the area is also home to other classic wooden boats, such as the Essex fishing smack. These were among the finest fishing vessels of their time, equipped with boomed gaff mainsails and cutter-rigged headsails, of which the jib is set flying from a thrusting bowsprit. The smack evolved to an almost perfect shape because of the need to get home quickly with the day's catch, the rig enabling fast and efficient sailing up the river and in and out of the creeks. Originally they had transom sterns, but to increase deck space the distinctive counter-stern, as beautiful as it was functional, was designed.

It was under power of sail alone that fishermen from waterside towns and villages such as West Mersea, Tollesbury, Maldon and Bradwell worked these smacks. A common scenario was backing the foresail while having a reef in the mainsail. This allowed the boat to drift with the tide, slowly scouring the river bed with iron oyster dredges. Sometimes they would shoot nets over the bulwark in search of sprat, herring or shrimp, or scour a creek bed for a bushel or two of winkles. In doing so, for centuries these men placed a fish supper on Britain's tables.

Maldon smack Lizzie Annie *can often be seen sailing in the Blackwater. She was built at Brightlingsea in 1906.*

Most smack owners today maintain these fine craft in tip-top condition and race them regularly in classic boat regattas. The traditional skills of handling a classic workboat while fishing under sail are also kept alive with events such as the annual oyster dredging match, which is held off Mersea Island, home to a particularly large number of smacks.

The beach huts at Mill Beach overlook Blackwater Bay. Millbeach Marine Club and slipway are on right of the picture.

Today's cruise was planned making full use of the tide, which would enable *Huffler* to crawl along some very shallow creeks on the way up to the causeway at Fullbridge, Maldon. A force 3 north-westerly wind was blowing as I rounded Decoy Point and headed over to the moorings at Mill Beach. The previous night I had camped at Decoy Creek in the saltings, eventually drying out in the mud. *Huffler* had become stuck while trying to position her and she had settled with a severe heel, which meant a restless night leaning against the centre plate casing. Rubbing a still sleepy eye while taking up a kneeling stance at the helm, I readied about for a concentrated beat through the many moored yachts ahead, finally sailing into Saltcote Creek.

It amuses me that when I enter a shallow creek, and need to be more cautious with the depth, I somehow seem to be lost on the beauty and wonderment of the new surroundings.

The enchanting close-boarded hut of the Saltcote Sailing Club here was a distraction because the boat had come to a standstill, stuck on a mud shoal. The only other clubs you can sail alongside the building is Dabchicks at West Mersea or Maldon Yacht Club, but I can't think of

Entering Saltcote Creek, the creek is split in two by an island of saltmarsh and bounded one side by the wharf of one of the prettiest little sailing clubs around, Saltcote Sailing Club. The former maltings are to the left of this picture. To the right, just the other side of the seawall a tide mill once worked, though long since demolished, but the mill pond remains.

another clubhouse on the Blackwater that has its own wharf; a wonderful little club.

The boat soon began to float again, so I continued on, reaching the wreck of a motor-torpedo boat on the port side close to the converted maltings. The sailing barge *Saltcote Belle* was built in Maldon by Howard in 1895 to work out of the mill here. She would have docked here for loading of malt before heading off to London.

The building has now been converted very sympathetically into flats. Pushing *Huffler* away from the bank with the paddle, her two headsails filled to take us back out of the creek. Almost mischievously we crossed the shallow water of the Ballast Hole heading south east and sailed past a number of Sprite clinker dinghies as they tugged at their moorings. There are around 30 of these classic little one-design 14 footers at Blackwater Sailing Club, and many of them turn out to race. But they look like an ideal little cruising dinghy.

Previously when I had passed Northey Island this year I had either been too early or too late to explore the inviting shallow entrance into Awl Creek, one of three creeks up-river that rarely feels the prodding of a

Saltcote Creek. The wreck of a motor torpedo boat or MTB part buried in the mud. Just the other side of the saltmarsh bank on the right is the Ballast Hole where another hulk can be found.

Northey Island. Reaching along Awl Creek in a good six feet of water. The hulks of Mistley *and* Gillman *are ahead on the saltings.*

visiting keel on its muddy surface. The other two are Saltcote Creek, from where we have just come, and Heybridge Creek. At Hilly Pool Point on Northey there is a short-cut. The opening in the bank of the island's northern corner is getting bigger due to erosion. I had timed the tide well, being able to bump *Huffler* over the eroded seawall entrance and into the deeper water of the creek. I eased the mainsheet and staysail and *Huffler* settled on a steady course, moving along slowly. Among the surrounding marshes, whimbrel and plover sat singing beside the sea aster. A small number of little egret were also dotted about and the unmistakable sound of the oystercatcher seemed to get louder the further along the creek we went. Looking across the narrow strip of grassy bank that separates Awl Creek from the main river, I caught sight of the helm of a yacht. He was turning his head again and again, and I assumed he must have been taking a second look, as the vision before him resembled a boat sailing on the seawall. Moments later I had reached the remains of two barges, *Mistley* and *Gillman* where I paused for a moment at a sharp turn eastward. From here it is possible to continue further into the saltmarsh and eventually exit north-east of the island. I carefully pushed off *Mistley*, her decaying hulk moaning, readying *Huffler* about, while birds sung, screeching and piping as if to warn their human visitor. I guided *Huffler* back northwards to sail quietly along the western stretch of the creek, exiting back through the earlier entry point and into Collier's Reach.

Things were looking good today, one of those all-to-infrequent escapades when everything seems to be coming together. As I passed Stebbings Boatyard, followed soon after by the sailing barge *Decima* sitting on the mud beside CRS Marine, the sun now shone across the bows of moored yachts at the Wilkin tearooms. Red-topped withie markers pointed the way towards the Heybridge lock gates, which is where 14 miles of fresh water canal merges with sea water.

Even further inland the Blackwater rises in a north-westerly direction through rambling countryside becoming stream-like where it is called The Pant. Bounded by chestnut trees and large oaks The Pant begins approximately 400 feet above sea level, just south-east of the medieval Essex market town of Saffron Walden.

Along with the River Chelmer and smaller tributaries, these two rivers are the very source of the Blackwater.

Heybridge Basin lock gates. Two pairs of gates operate at the lock. The outer pair hold back the sea while the inner gates retain the calmer water of the Chelmer & Blackwater Canal.

Inside, the Basin retains an ambience of bygone days with wooden waterside cottages and a collection of boats moored in flat calm water. It was once a very busy dock with shipbreakers and boatbuilders, and lots of timber coming in on barge lighters which was offloaded from large Baltic ships anchored down river at Osea.

A few people were sitting on the seawall by the two pubs, the Ship Inn and the Jolly Sailor. Two hulks were on the mud passed the lock gates at Metes Hard and I then got the first glimpse of Maldon as the barge *Nellie*, with her short stumpy rig, sailed by. I gripped the tiller and made good progress towards the town, steering close to the navigation buoys until abreast the statue of Bryhtnoth. The Maldon Yacht Club occupies a quaint little corner of the river here, their clubhouse built on top of a steel barge lighter. Just below, in an area of saltings, a few decaying clinker wrecks typify the mix of old and new that make up the special charm of this area of the Essex coastline. I sailed off to starboard crossing the river and inside the Back Channel opposite, right up beside the pair of hulks, *Scotia*, an iron pot and *Oxygen*, which is wooden and the sistership *to Hydrogen*. From the saltings here is an unfamiliar view of Maldon and The Hythe.

To reach certain shallow corners of the river I will often risk grounding the boat by sailing in too early, but only on the flood. This time I freed a stuck rudder and centreboard by snatching at *Huffler's* lines, while shuffling about from side to side. I got back to the main channel where one of the most photographed of fishing smacks, in recent years, *Telegraph*, is moored.

A small stretch of seawall to port hides a small lake, until recently a bathing area. This area was called the Bath Wall by the many smacksmen who left their boats here. Their booms were left hanging towards the wall so that the boat would lay upwards on the sloping bank at low tide.

It was close to high water neaps on this beautiful sunny morning and the quayside was packed with barges, all looking immaculately turned out. Two of the barges were full of day-trippers readying for a passage.

I counted six working barges rafted at the quay, not including barge *Xylonite*, which sat on the blocks at Cooks Yard. The blocks enable a barge to sit above the mud at low tide so her underside can be inspected or worked on. On another occasion I have counted nine working barges at The Hythe.

The Saxon-meaning for Hythe is Haven, which is an appropriate word as this spot has become a centre for anyone interested in preserving these traditional boats. I tacked across river and back almost brushing against the sailing barge *Wyvenhoe's* iron top sides. Surprisingly there were no cruisers moored on the visitors' quay so, taking full advantage, I guided *Huffler's* little bow towards the wall, tucking in behind *Kitty* and *Thistle* and tied up before taking some refreshments.

More often than not you can find yourself sailing alongside a barge out on the main river, and it is always a treat to see these huge spritsail craft at home in this relaxed setting. Dwarfed by these old-timers I hopped out onto the quayside for a closer look.

It was a stirring sight. A forest of masts and spars towered above, all draped by huge flanks of ochre-tanned canvas. A mass of ropes strung fore and aft, way up high to the topmasts, wooden deadeyes were roved and seized fast, brightly painted decks had caulking bursting through their joins. Red hawser pipe popped through bow badges, names were carved, painted yellow into the broad transoms, off which shaped rudders hung like statues. The muddy waters of the mornings rising tide swirled around their splintered timbers.

Maldon is still a working barge dock today, though the cargo may be different in the way of the paying day-tripper whose fascination for these wonderful craft helps maintain their tradition.

Our streets are now full with motor vehicles with a thirst for fuel, the price of which continues to rise each year. Traffic jams are getting longer and our roads have never been more congested, added to the fact there is now worldwide concerns over greenhouse gasses filling the air. Mass transporting of goods via an eco-friendly sailing craft has never looked more appealing. Who knows, one day we may have to give the Thames sailing barge a second look, in search of a design for its modern equivalent, and a rebirth of industrial cargo being moved under a harnessed power of sail, along our coasts and up our rivers and creeks?

Just up the hill there is the pretty high street containing a good variety of little shops. There is also a pie-and-mash shop that makes the liquor just right, unfortunately I am not able to visit today; time and tide waits for no-one.

Climbing aboard and releasing *Huffler's* lines, my little boat drifted silently away from the quayside. Above The Hythe, the historic Shipways Yard caters for many yachts, as does Landbreach and the Downes Road Boatyard, which has a number of tidal mud berths. Further along here the river is a calm oasis behind the urban facade of houses whose back gardens reach to the water's edge. I had arrived at the limit of the Blackwater and the entrance to Heybridge Creek.

I could see the shapely metal hull of the sailing barge *Portlight*. She was built at Mistley in 1925 and now lay moored among other large lighter hulls that sit inside the creek mouth.

In Heybridge Creek. The former Sadd's wharf is to the left.

I entered this creek slowly and with caution and made for the piled metal fencing that rose out of the creek on my port side. Searching the depths with the cane showed I was in a couple of feet of water. The creek is no more than five or six feet deep at best, if you are able to keep in the narrow gut. The wind, though light, was flukey and uncertain for a few moments due to that fact I was being enclosed by a steel lighter to starboard. But I was still just able to sail further into the creek, flanked by chainlink and concrete fencing, behind which large factory buildings towered above the creek. *Huffler's* own metal intermittently knocked loudly. Something large and hard was beneath, a submerged trolley or a pedal bike? I did not like the sound of this and risked being holed if I continued. I looked south-east in search of the deeper gut but was taken in by the beautiful saltmarsh that spreads all the way down towards Northey Island. To port, just over the high concrete wall, was a piece of industrial wasteland. The deserted former wharf of John Sadd & Sons. The Sadds had their own fleet of barges that would have been docked all around these walls, either unloading timber for their own busy sawmills or other products the firm handled. From 1831 this was one of the busiest wharfs in Maldon with shipping coming in and out from the Baltic Sea. Sadds was also the second largest employer in Maldon and, like other

Heybridge Creek at low water. Sadd's slipway in the foreground. The saltings and new housing development are further up the creek.

yards in the river, produced motor-torpedo boats during the war. With the amount of work going on up-river for the war effort, it is no wonder that at this time an iron defence boom was strung across the river lower down, from Shinglehead Point over to Bradwell. Today, however, Heybridge Creek is a quiet backwater, though there are plans to regenerate this site with a new housing development.

I drifted on under jib and paddle past a ghostly iron rail track that ran down from the wharf into the creek. I was now beside more familiar saltmarsh, just floating, in very shallow water where a few house boats are moored and two rotting barge hulks *Edith* and *Hilda* have blended into the saltings. One of the hulks has a carpet of marsh grass and a rusted iron aga stove that stands upright as if just waiting for someone to put a kettle on. I could not go any further, for a new housing development was just over the seawall ahead, so we scuttled off back down the creek, the wind dying while in the lee of the wall. Paddling to get back out into the Chelmer, I persisted with trying to sail the boat. I tacked past two gentlemen on a motor-launch and one called over "I admire your stamina." Just then the wind blew over *Huffler's* deck, filling her headsails and sending us bowling along up to the bridge.

We passed the black boarded building of the Maldon Crystal Salt Works on the way up, followed by some more houseboats and then a large coaster and the sailing barge *Lady Jean* sitting to port against Fullbridge wharf. A building here with a shrimp carved into the brickwork over its doorways is the former warehouse of a brewer of Shrimp Brand Beers who were based in Gravesend. The brewers had a small fleet of barges that would bring beer to Maldon as well as other East Coast ports.

A beer brewing connection can be found today just up the hill from here at Silver Street where the Maldon Brewing Co Ltd is based. To starboard was Green's flour mill building, still a busy mill where giant coasters can often be seen at the wharf unloading grain. Ahead, and at the limit of this adventure, the bridge where The River Chelmer continues to wind its way inland. Who knows, maybe next time I will be venturing beyond into the deep of the Chelmer countryside..?

Green's flower mill and wharf. There is usually a large coaster or two beside the quay here at Fullbridge

"I downed sails and paddled with the remaining flood
deep into the confines of this tiny creek"

Chapter Six
Creek Harvest

CYCLING down the narrow lane to the creek an unusual roar of machinery could be heard coming from close by. Intrigued, I peddled a little quicker, but was unable to see what noise was disturbing the usual sweet music of the surrounding countryside, the perpetrator being behind the cover of a row of dense bushes. On reaching the end of the lane and having climbed the seawall, a cloud of dust washed over me. I felt as if I had been caught in a desert storm, the sandy-coloured dust and strands of straw covering both myself and my cycle. Large amounts of dust settled on the surface of the water, but fortunately a gusty wind blowing in off the river quickly cleared the air. Looking beyond the wall to the adjacent fields I could see some farmers and a huge combine-harvester gathering wheat, a sure sign that the high summer's sailing season was nearly over. Brushing myself down, I thought it only right to do a bit of harvesting myself, but aboard *Huffler*. After wading through mud and incoming tide, I arrived at the boat and quickly removed her canvas cover, and readied her sails for the three days of pocket cruising that lay ahead. The wind was gusting force 5-6, kicking up a nasty chop in Goldhanger Creek, but by the time I let go the mooring I was able to reach across the entrance under reefed main and staysail in a somewhat calmer sea state. Reaching the now covered Earl Creek I readied about to head over to Wilkin's saltings. It was just a few weeks earlier that I had watched the fruit pickers harvesting the famous jam-maker's berries just below the seawall. Like the wheat harvest, it is a pleasing sight, though a stark reminder that summer's warm grip was loosening. I readied about beside the ancient wooden structure that sits at the mouth of Wilkin's Creek. It was jutting up menacingly six inches above the surface, so I quickly fetched across

All set for a comfortable night in Cooper's Creek, a favourite hideaway.

Ford Creek towards the red No 4 buoy marking the entrance to Southey Creek. My route took me north and well wide of Osea Island's western tip. With only two or three other boats out on the water, this was great sailing. One of them was the Thames barge *Decima*, which lay at anchor in the Latchingdon Hole on Osea's southern shore. *Decima* was built of steel in 1899 to work out of Grays in Essex and as of 2011 her tops'l can be seen displaying the 'Tiptree' logo of her local sponsor.

The westerly wind was backing south-westerly, seemingly following *Huffler's* bow wherever it pointed.

From the Southey Creek buoy I was able to hold a compass course south and sailed into the shallow entrance to Cooper's Creek, which is one of my favourite haunts up river. On entering the creek, its wide mouth quickly narrows and forks in two directions, vein-like into a maze of saltmarsh, deserted and captivating. Taking the western fork, I downed sails and paddled with the remaining flood deep into the confines of this tiny creek. Up high on the flood tide I had a clear view across the saltings. The tufted grasses of the saltings were painted with the sun's late evening glow, creating shades of fawny gold. Beyond, I could clearly see *Decima*, still anchored off Osea Island, and, on glancing eastwards, the distant concrete fortress of Bradwell, a contrast that provided an evocative surreal scene. The narrowing soft marshy banks bumped and funnelled *Huffler* along as her bow gently nosed them from side to side until we reached a narrow gut where we sat perfectly cushioned by eel grass for a contented night among the marsh wildlife.

A Creeksailor's classic, Cooper's Creek.

The following morning's high tide was at a very decent 0719 hrs, which meant I was able to paddle back down the creek at 0550 hrs and, encouraged by a fantastic sunrise and the lightest of airs, I took the flood up the wider eastern fork of the creek. I was able to tack to the very top and back, often needing to raise *Huffler's* centre-plate and rudder, but I had time still to repeat the voyage before heading out of the creek. With 15 minutes of morning flood left, I entered Lawling Creek and landed at the beautiful beach of Mundon Stone Point.

Dropping the anchor onto the soft sand I climbed out and gave the little pocket ships mud-strewn sides a good clean. Continuing east, the impressive Stansgate Abbey Farm, home of the former Cabinet Minister

Anchored just inside Lawling Creek at Mundon Stone Point. The water to the right of the point is the main river.

Tony Benn that dominates the landscape, was in full view, providing a good course to steer to enter Steeple Creek where the saltings were washed by the high tide. The wind, being westerly, made a deep entrance to explore the whole creek unadvisable so I took advantage of the rising breeze and enjoyed a decent beat back along seawall below the remains of Stansgate Abbey. In the year 1112AD this spot was a sanctuary for Cluniac Monks and, like The Chapel of St Peter-on-the-Wall at Bradwell, must once have been a desolate and solitary outpost.

Passing Marconi Sailing Club, I began counting the WW2 pill boxes that dot the shore and was able to ease the mainsail out for a steaming run down river inside the moorings. The concrete hard of the Marconi Sailing Club is one of 68 built around the coast during the war and the pretty little white shed that sits up on the seawall was once a wash house, built for officers and their families that were placed on a watch vessel guarding this stretch of river in the 19th century. The seawall here also hides The Wade, a forgotten creek that lays behind it.

The Wash House at Marconi Sailing Club hard.

At high spring tides, water would have encircled Ramsey Island from this creek across marshland towards St Lawrence Bay.

At 0839 hrs I passed the deep water moorings at Stone Sailing Club, still just an hour after high water, I had already visited eight creeks when another gem came into view just past the old transit markers at Transit Creek. Suddenly the entrance to St Lawrence Creek was beneath me. Why take the easy route of the main river when the opportunity of navigating a magic creek that lay to my starboard side was so close by?

As I pushed away the tiller and pulled in *Huffler's* mainsail to reach in towards the rolling green hillside of St Lawrence Bay, I took to the sounding pole, preferring the direct contact feeling it gives in the more critical depths of a creek. Turning eastwards again onto a run, *Huffler's* sails filled nicely. We were now charging down the creek, though we passed a metal pole just visible on my starboard side cautiously. Sail south of this pole and you are on the mudflats; sail into it and you are probably going to be holed and sunk. Continuing towards the large tinkling yacht masts in the calm of Bradwell Creek, *Huffler* soon glided passed Pewet Island with its Nature Reserve and abundant bird life singing in the chorus of the new day. Somehow I managed to keep a steady course between the island and the moored yachts, the very peak of *Huffler's* gaff waggling happily, tail-like while we charge gloriously along. The Doomsday book of 1086 refers to this creek being called Hacflet, which in old English stands for creek with a bend. I was soon round this dog's hind leg of a turn at the island's eastern tip, scraping the plate over the mud before gybing and sailing back out of the creek to the Bradwell power station Baffle. Creek-crawling can be thirsty work and a constant hydration process via a brew is one way to keep alert so, pulling in *Huffler's* mainsail, I reached passed the tide pole and crossed the river to Mell Creek, which was by now just running dry. Just beside the remains of the old pier I dropped anchor to rest for a while in the heat of the early morning sun.

The remains of Tollesbury pier. Mell Creek entrance can be made out left of centre in this image. The area around Mell Creek is littered with hard shingle shoals, although inside lots of soft mud can be found.

The pier was linked to the Crab and Winkle line that once ran to Tollesbury and down to the river terminus. The small railway line was intended to bring life into this remote part of Essex but the pier soon fell into disrepair after the line was disbanded and its eventual demise came after a large part of it was destroyed during the war when it was used as part of the defence measures against possible invasion. With mainsail reefed, I pulled up the anchor and stowed it below in the tiny cabin ready for immediate use. Unhurriedly, *Huffler* drifted on the tide while I sat relaxed, observing the scenery slowly passing by. Now close in to the shoal shore I freed off on to a run and in no time reached The Nass, creeping gingerly over the mud shoal into Thornfleet Creek and passing Pennyhole Creek and Sunken Island to port. There was still a couple of hours of ebb to run, so I fired up the outboard motor to help my passage through this pretty but tricky stretch of water.

There are around a thousand moorings at Mersea where on a weekend The Quarters can have its busy moments, a bit like the spaghetti junction of the waterways with boats coming and going from rows of moorings that shoot off in all directions lining the deeper water of the fleets.

Packing Marsh Island and its famous local landmark the Packing Shed. Shelter from strong winds can be found in the lee of the islands, when cruising the deeper creeks around Mersea Quarters.

Boats of all descriptions sit beside Coast Road at boatyards such as West Mersea Marine or Peter Clarke's. One can also delight in seeing a small wooden shed with nearby oyster pits still being worked. Live music can be heard in the Coast Inn and further down the long established Gowen Ocean Sailmakers can be found. For a taste of the sea Native oysters dredged from the surrounding creeks can be eaten when there is an R in the month, and can be found alongside other fresh fish in the Company Shed or the Oyster Bar. The shingle beach of the Packing Shed Island with its barge hulk, *Fanny*, looked inviting, as did the church tower of St Peter and St Paul.

Monkey Beach. The church tower of St peter and St Paul on the high ground. King's Hard is in the distance. Note the pillbox in the sand centre of the picture and the boulders to seaward that cover. Gunfleet Sands wind farm is in the far distance on the right.

The restored sailing barge, *Dawn,* lay further up the creek moored on a pile mooring. Large fishing vessels swung from huge buoys, the hards were a hive of activity, and children dangled crabbing lines off the pontoon beside a raft of skiffs. I resisted the temptation to grab a cuppa and baguette special from The Blackwater Pearl cafe and dropped anchor beside the wreck of a smack *Rosetta*, which was used to bring potatoes from the Channel Islands. In 1914 the Tollesbury and Mersea Oyster Company bought the Island. Around this time Packing Shed was a hive of activity with up to 60 fishermen sorting the oysters that were brought here. Once cleaned and packed they were taken to London by barge. The Shed eventually fell into disrepair after a decline in oyster fishing in the 1950s. Having become such an important part of the landscape, a group of local people got together in 1990 to restore it and formed The Packing Shed Trust. Work began in 1991 and the building was reopened in its former glory in 1992. The trust continue to maintain this historic building

Anchored in Ray Creek. The small forest of dense bushes is Ray Island.

today. Just across Mersea Creek and the green capped Cobmarsh Island was Besom Creek, where possibly one of the oldest boats still sailing, *Boadicia*, can be seen. She was built at Maldon in 1808 as an oyster smack so is now over 200 years old. Other smacks also line the creek swinging from mooring buoys that are controlled by Victory Moorings.

From the steep to golden sand and shingle around Hove Creek Beach the tiny Hove Creek reaches across St Peter's Well Meadow that crowns this end of the handsome Monkey Beach.

On a flat calm day I have beached the pocket ship here for either a walk along the beach or a climb up Monkey Steps to look at St Peter's Well, a natural spring that was once one of the island's main source of water. This area of Coast Road enjoys stunning views across the estuary. A short walk up the hill to the island's museum is also well worth a look.

It was nice to just sit and watch the boats go by for a while, but other creeks beckoned. I lifted the anchor and motored up the creek. Once passed the piles, I cut the engine and sailed quietly up the Ray, anchoring in the deep mud just outside the entrance to Sampson's Creek, and wandered over the remains of the sailing barge *Unity*. From the seawall the farmland of Feldy marshes spread out towards Copt Hall and Salcott.

Removing the mud from my boots I resumed the pleasant sail over what was left of the ebb up to Ray Island. The small golden beach contrasted with the green leaves of the thorn trees that dominate Ray Island and are such a pleasing sight to the eye. An oasis for wildlife and visiting boats seeking solitude just above the busy fleets of West Mersea, Ray Island was also the home of the fictional character in the Reverend Sabine Baring-Gould's tragic melodrama, Mehalah. A beautiful but fiery young woman who lived with her gin-fuelled mother. Their peaceful and idyllic existence on the island was shattered by the unwanted advances of evil landlord Elijah Rebow, whose lust for power is only matched by his desire for Mehalah. The island is owned by The National Trust and managed by Essex Wildlife Trust.

While anchored at the small sandy beach by the wreck I had plenty of time to enjoy the surroundings as I cooked a filling lunch of new potatoes and asparagus. Afterwards, as I lay on my bunk with the boat gently rocking at anchor, my thoughts turned to the creeks I had visited earlier. I got out my own hand-drawn map, on which I had marked each place visited on this small cruise so far. With the warmth of the sun penetrating the companionway I drifted into a well-earned sleep. On awakening I noticed the flood was well on its way in and *Huffler's* anchor had dragged. I quickly readied the sails and took the tide just a little further around a bend into the narrowing Peldon Creek, where we stuck firm in the mud. Luckily we were soon floating again and continued on, to the top of the creek. The private residence beside the creek here was once visited by barge lighters that would unload limpet shells for a small firm once based here who crushed and sold them as chicken grit. Unable to go any further, I spun the little ship around and sailed over the incoming tide, past Bonner's saltings and down Ray Creek. Winding through the withies and keeping out of the main flood, I passed Feldy Creek and Little Ditch, rounded into Salcott Channel where the western bank is proliferated with inlets and rills that lead into saltings and a number of small oyster pits. This area is also known locally as Syphon Creek for it was here a barge landed with Isambard Kingdom Brunel's Syphon. Once up past the moorings and Sunken Island, the magnificence of this lovely stretch of water was evident, allowing me to make some long tacks through a maze of withies that mark out the oyster layings.

Exploring the upper reaches of the longest creek in the Blackwater, Salcott Creek. The creek has many turns and is predominantly bounded by marsh and farmland.

The views of Peldon up on the hill and the church tower above Copt Hall Creek are delightful. Nosing *Huffler's* bow into the saltings at Abbotts Hall Creek, we continued on, passing to starboard a disused farm dock. It was a remote spot and a solitary *Huffler* that closed in on the breached seawall opposite Quinces corner, the first bend of Salcott Creek. It seems ironic that in the early 19th century engineer I K Brunel who designed steamships, suspension bridges, tunnels and viaducts, came to this area to install a water syphon, which drained sea water from the flooding marshes into Salcott Creek. But today we are doing the opposite. In the distance I could see more combine-harvesters working busily. I could not have painted a better picture of this historical link between the farmer's plough and the mariner's sail. As the combines disappeared into the distance, I could hear the cows mooing contentedly, a sound interrupted only by the scraping of *Huffler's* plate on mother earth. I had reached my mud anchorage where I would dry out for the night. I let go the sheets and reached over to prod with the sounding cane.

Using the sounding cane in Salcott Creek. This method of sounding was learnt years earlier from the Grand Master of the art, Charlie Stock.

With an hour-and-a-half to high water there was 2 foot of water beneath us. Continuing up this snaking creek, I passed a remote bird-watcher's hide It was a moment to cherish, so down came the sails and we drifted, deliberately slowly. This was not a voyage I wanted to end. We were deep into this sizeable creek, one that epitomises everything about the kind of sailing I love; being afloat on a small boat surrounded by so many natural elements with new adventures around every twist and turn, the secrets unfolding before you. From here, this little world really is the proverbial oyster, a world of childhood dreams as one might read in the tales of Enid Blyton's Famous Five or Arthur Ransom's Swallows and Amazons, outdoors and cooking over make-do fires, all huddled cosily in a small space. I awoke suddenly from my day-dreaming. It was now 1837 hrs and high water was at 1954 hrs, and I had ran aground, my concentrating wavering while at the helm as I stretched on tip-toe to peer over the seawall at the top of emerging bastion of Salcott-cum-Virley church tower.

Church Wharf, Salcott. The wharf is at the rear of St Mary the Virgin church. The building survived an earthquake that shook this peaceful hamlet in 1884, bringing to ruins the nearby church of Virley.

Using my paddle against the bank, I was able to reverse down a little to anchor beside an old mooring. Taking a reading from the sounding pole, it showed that there was just over 2 feet here so, using the time wisely, I put the kettle on for a cuppa and waited patiently. The fruits of my labour were yet unreachable around the next bend; so near but teasingly still not navigable due to the lack of water. A stab with the sounding pole at 1945 hrs read 3 feet 2 inches, which meant I had another foot of water further up, just enough to enable *Huffler* to float. With minutes left to high tide, I clawed my way through the tiny cabin and reached through the forehatch to raise the muddy anchor. As I returned to the cockpit and hoisted the yard, a gentle evening breeze filled the tanned mainsail. With the rigging creaking, I unfurled the jib and began the final leg of a magical journey. Tiller in one hand and sounding cane in the other, I rounded another narrow bend. This time with about 3 foot of water in the middle of the creek. The magic hour was now upon us, the sun's golden glow at its best. I took *Huffler's* tiny bow around the final narrow bend, in the footsteps of the old men of sail to where the Church of St Mary stood.

Picturesque Church Wharf, Salcott. This is the navigable limit of the creek due to a dam. But the creek continues the other side passing through pretty gardens.

This wondrous creek had taken us from the choppy seas at the mouth of the estuary right into the very heart of this tiny hamlet of Salcott-cum-Virley. Above the creek's grassy bank the pretty church tower was lit, poetically, by the glow, as was the old barge wharf that sat at the water's edge. As two ponies grazed the bank, I savoured the moment before me. More recently a staging has been built here but in the days when sailing barges would bring up here they would have dropped anchor, with just a board from the hold straight onto the land, and offloaded the cargo ashore in iron-wheeled barrows. Some barges had to be helped through these awkward bends by a Huffler, a local skipper who knew the water and its shallow depths.

Once there were two pubs serving this village, a fact that reflects its importance as a busy rural dock. Mersea men would also come up for a day's sail on a spring tide and anchor at the top while they had a pint. After a little paddling to manoeuvre the boat about the dock, I made my way back to the mud mooring for a night in the mud. Later, having rustled up an evening meal, I sat beneath the stars in the cockpit sipping a celebratory glass of beer soaking in the solitude and the peaceful lowing of the neighbouring herd.

The morning after in Salcott Creek.

At 0535 hrs the following morning, *Huffler* floated and, with the wind in the west, I was able to sail back down the creek and out through the Quarters, enjoying an exciting wind-over-tide beat back up river and deliberately taking the Thirslet Creek route to my mooring at Goldhanger. The creek takes you north-west around the Thirslet Spit and over shallow ground above Collin's Creek where there are two iron wrecks that were once used for target practice by WW2 fighter planes.

On the way I caught sight of some small black summer lambs on the seawall by Joyce's Creek, so I decided to sail in and anchor just inside at the end of the spit and watch them play in the morning sunshine. A truly memorable harvest of creeks.

"I sailed a little further down river,
where there was another forgotten place"

Chapter Seven
In Search Of The Red Hills

IT WAS a pleasant late afternoon with warm hazy sunshine as I left my mooring in Goldhanger Creek. Sailing down river over the remaining flood tide I watched the yellow buoys that mark the Maldon Oyster & Seafood Company's layings, disappear in *Huffler's* wake. Keeping close to the shallow north shore, I scoured every indentation, *Huffler's* bowsprit, nosing in like a sniffer dog, looking for signs of abandoned wrecks, mooring posts or ancient seawall and fishing structures.

There are many stumps that stick up at various states of tide, so it could be considered quite a risky business venturing so close to the shore. Just like the withies, the barge hulks and the broken chunks of seawall, they all add to the very character of the Blackwater.

I soon reached Gore Saltings and Skinner's Wick, guiding *Huffler* into the area of an old farm wharf along the eastern seawall. Waterlogged bits of wood covered by weed broke the mirrored surface of this forgotten place. Just over the western seawall there are also small mounds of marsh grass that disguise a red hill.

The saltings here are a marvellous hideaway. Summer evenings spent drifting around in here are truly memorable. Even on rainy days, when the main river is windswept and blowing a gale, there is no better place to be tucked up inside the cabin with the tea brewing, peering out through the companionway.

A quiet backwater, Gore Saltings is at the head of Thirslet Creek. The wooden structure in the foreground was used by wildfowlers to access the saltings. Its condition is pretty good in relation to other wooden objects that can be found here, even though it shows the wear and tear of many tides. Beyond the island of saltmarsh the extending spit on the right is a continuation of Bulham beach. Deeper water can be found near to the east seawall which is to the left in this image.

I continued on to the mouth of Rolls Creek, my intended destination for the night. The creek looked inviting, with enough water to still get in, the evening sun lighting up the eastern bank where the deeper water can be found. Before heading into the creek I sailed a little further down river, where there was another forgotten place, Thistly Hard. Here there is a tiny beach in the bend of the seawall. I gripped *Huffler's* tiller tightly as we moved cautiously forward, for I knew that close in there were a line of stumps, which at one time would have formed the dock but today they were still below the water line. I hurriedly steered towards the deeper water when I felt the centre-board scrape against the shingle bottom.

Farm tracks at Thistly. You can almost guarantee that wherever a farm track reached the seawall a spritsail barge would have at one point in time landed there.

Drying out in Rolls Creek, a forgotten creek that provides the small-boat sailor with shelter from the main river. The many stumps that can be found in here signal that the creek was once often used.

This was a lonely place, though looking south, about a mile away I could just see a fleet of racing dinghies buzzing about off The Stone. My immediate concern was to get *Huffler* into the creek before the light faded as I had some exploring to do. The surrounding countryside is punctuated with farm cart tracks leading to the water's edge where barges once came to deliver and load, and Thistly is a good example.

Covered by seaweed, wood remains at Thistly Hard. Across the river St Lawrence Bay is to the south. Apart from these potential hazards, it is a nice shingle beach, good for landing and from where this picture was taken.

I made my way back into Rolls Creek, which sits between Rolls Farm and Decoy Farm, and was able to position *Huffler* in front of the small beach that is just inside. Using both anchors to hold us fast, we dried out in a perfect spot for the night. This tiny creek provides good shelter and the delightful beach is topped with cockleshells. But what I like most about visiting here is the advantage of being able to get ashore, for this is red hill country.

Before leaving the boat there was just enough time for a fish supper washed down with a glass of wine. I had timed my visit here to coincide with the ploughing of the fields and to provide enough evening sunshine for a long walk along the seawall, which gives fine views of the three ancient red hills that sit beside the creek. Much of the seawall along here has reclaimed saltmarsh for farming, so at one time the red hills would have been at the very water's edge.

Essex County Council, which keeps a record of the hills, says they are a distinctive feature of the Essex coastal landscape, and are not confined to the Blackwater. The red hills are mounds of ancient industrial waste from pottery vessels, ash and soil reddened by hot fires used to evaporate sea water, therefore leaving salt. The hills were formed about 2000 years ago all along the Essex coast which, we now know, has been a major salt-making industry since Roman times.

Beginning my evening walk along the seawall, it wasn't long before I could clearly recognise a couple of the hills. Many of the old hills have been inadvertantly ploughed back into the earth, which has improved the soil for today's crop-growing. And while many of the sites have disappeared, other hills are clearly visible, especially immediately after ploughing. Just past Rolls Farm was a particular site I had come to look at. A walk across the saltmarsh and a step down onto the small beach takes you into a red hill. At the water's edge, set in the 'cant' (the miniature cliff like edge of the saltings) large pieces of red pottery stick out, made visible by the eroding sea water. This is one of two fantastic sites inside the river that clearly shows thousands of years of salt production set in the layers of earth. There are also red hills on the southern shore of the river at places like St Lawrence, Steeple and Bradwell.

From this ancient salt making industry local names such as Salcott and Saltcote have come about, the demise in the salt-making industry came from competition with inland salt production that made the gathering of sea salt no longer profitable.

The Maldon Crystal Salt Company is now the only survivor of the Essex sea salt industry. I sat on the 'cant' looking out into the river, the sun had gone down in the west, leaving in its purple hazed wake glowing red streaks. Quite fitting. I walked back along the seawall in darkness, the warm air rising mistily off the water.

The following morning, heartened by a favourable forecast, I sailed out of the river mouth for an open-water sail of six or seven miles to the Wallet Spitway buoy and the Swin, then back, with the tide, and into the magical Blackwater.

Two photographs of a red hill near Rolls Creek.
With pieces of pottery set in the 'cant', this red hill brings to life another age.

Chapter Eight
Lawling, Mayland, Mundon and Steeple Creeks

I AWOKE to the faint sound of the tide rippling along the outside of the boat. Immediately I smiled, it was a friendly sound that I could never tire from hearing. The night had been a cold one and the sea state bumpy but I had been tucked up in the cabin with two sleeping bags. The boat had been swinging from her anchor in readiness for a spot of creek-crawling up river. High water was not until the afternoon, so I decided to head into Lawling Creek on the flood. The mouth of the creek is directly opposite the pier on Osea Island. Most of the upper creek dries but there is usually enough water left to get up by the marina, unless during the lowest of spring tides. Steeple Creek lay towards the east across a wide stretch of mud that was still sitting high and dry, though nearer high water this easterly wind means a nice beat into the creek where there is plenty of

Steeple Creek. This area was known as Bay Creeks by Maldon fishermen.

saltmarsh found poking up through the surface of the water. With enough depth, you can find your way in near the north wall. If not, follow the marsh southward through a tight snaking bend. Steeple is neither a deep nor a lengthy creek, but nonetheless is very enjoyable. The area has been known as Canney Marshes and was well-known for its abundance of wildlife. From October it is not unusual to see an occasional wildfowler on the marshes, a good indication of just how idyllic it still is here. I have not dried out in Steeple as yet but I imagine it would be a quiet night. Having said that, on a warm summer's night holidaymaker's singing from the nearby caravan site can on occasion be heard across the river. One evening I heard this singing from the sanctuary of the north shore creeks, it does raise a smile.

Lawling Creek is a delightful place to spend some time; a mixture of seals, serenity and marshlands contrasts with the clamour and activity at Blackwater Marina and the two local sailing clubs, all of which come alive when the water is in. Soft mud can be found all around Mundon Stone Point, which is a delightful place to dry out if you are staying the night as there is a lovely little beach to explore. The seals, too, seem to like it here, and were not in the least bothered by our presence, seemingly more interested in sunning themselves.

Lawling Creek. Former Cardnell Brothers Boatyard, now Blackwater Marina. The Thames barge Gladys *can be seen in dry dock to the right.*

With the plate creaking along the bottom I crawled around the entrance to Mayland Creek, which branches off of Lawling Creek in a south-easterly direction. It is shallower here than inside the creek, and there is a slipway used by residents of the Steeple Bay Holiday Park. Sailing into the creek on the tide you will find a tranquil and peaceful corner of the Blackwater that stretches deep into rural Essex. The banks of the creek are natural saltmarsh, and you pass a very sharp S-bend, at which point a ditch branches off east towards Steeple Hall where there is a former barge dock. The dock has many wooden stumps and a small concrete hard. Opposite is a small island with enough water to navigate around. With just the sound of marsh birds filling the air the area is a useful mud anchorage if staying aboard overnight. At the top of the creek is a derelict wharf called Pigeon Dock. Spritsail barges such as the 45 ton *Mayland* and the 44 ton *Mundon* would have sailed up to this small dock where goods were transported by cart along Dock Road, which is no more than

Pigeon Dock, at the very tranquil head of Mayland Creek.

a narrow track. The mooring and dock area are now owned by friend and fellow small-boat sailor Brian Goodbourn. Back in Lawling Creek, I had to tack repeatedly so the centre-plate was used for soundings. Each time a scrape was heard I went about, pinching a little more ground each time. I find it great fun sailing in shallow water where you can see the mud just inches from your hull; almost teasing you. But all the while you know that even if you do touch you will be floating again very soon on the rising tide.

Lawling Creek. Seals can often be seen along the western bank.

The former barge dock at Brick House Farm in Lawling Creek. Cargo would have been stored in the area to the left which is encircled by raised walls. This protected area enabled farm cargo to be left without fear of damage from high spring tides while waiting collection from a barge. The timbers used for the dockside are still visible to the right, although these have eroded considerably in the last 15 years.

The western bank of the creek has some beautiful saltings that can be investigated near high tide. The inquisitive cruiser will find wooden remains of a farm dock where stack barges would have served Brick House Farm. What is particularly interesting about this former dock is how it is built. A row of stakes at the water's edge were anchored by two longer poles which reached inland to posts set into firm ground. The retaining stakes would have been backfilled to make a firm landing quay. This technique of small farm dock construction can be seen in one or two other rivers along the coast. The dock also has an area of grassland protected by a small raised earth wall which is similar to the Ship Lock at Abbots Hall Creek. These were built to protect produce from spring tides while awaiting collection by a barge.

From Harlow (Blackwater) Sailing Club the deeper water doglegs round to the Blackwater Marina where opposite I dropped anchor in soft mud. Although relatively shallow, Lawling is a main artery branching off the upper river, and a variety of boats can be seen here. The marina is the former site of the yacht building yard of Cardnell Brothers, which was called upon on by the Admiralty in WW2 to build torpedo and gun boats. Barges docked here in the days of working sail to transport cargo to and from London. Traditional boats rest beside modern yachts along the pontoons and there is often a barge undergoing work here. Recently the sailing barge *Gladys* has been tucked away in dry dock having some restoration work done. I have also seen classic fishing smacks such as the 41 foot Kings Lynn boat *Rob-Pete* and the little 31 foot Maldon smack *Joseph T* undergoing restoration.

Maylandsea Bay Sailing club is also based at the upper reach of Lawling. The club is home to the largest fleet of Sandhoppers in the area. With their distinctive blue sails and triple keels, they are a shallow draft version of the fin-keel Squib, designed by the prodigious Oliver J Lee. The Sandhopper is not only an ideal racing boat for these parts but is also ideal for cruising.

The area opposite the clubhouse becomes Mundon Creek where there is plenty to keep the small-boat sailor occupied. In the corner of the saltings is a wreck which is covered at high water.

Mundon Creek. The wreck is to the right by the tuft of saltmarsh. The creek continues past this solitary yacht mooring into remote saltmarsh.

I found this to my cost one day when I was in here at high water searching for the submerged wreck and I nearly lost my rudder when I scraped over it.

The creek here is not confined by narrow banks allowing you enough space to explore the fringes under sail in most wind directions. There are some low-level houses along the promenade from the club before the scenery turns into remote arable farmland. This stretch of seawall is part of the 45-mile St Peter's Way Walk, which starts at Chipping Ongar and finishes at the St Peter-on-the-Wall Chapel at Bradwell. The upper reach of Mayland Creek's eastern bank down to the Steeple Hall dock is also part of the walk.

It was time to move on, so raising sail and weighing anchor, my little boat made way gently down the creek, this time passing some dinghy sailors from Harlow (Blackwater) Sailing Club in the early stages of their racing on the rising tide. Boats are launched from a wooden jetty that reaches down into the creek. Their pretty clubhouse has views of the creek and up to Osea. On exiting the creek and scraping over Mundon Stone Point, I headed over to the north-west of Osea Island, it was a lively sail and, as I rounded the island I was treated to a majestic view down river, and beyond the horizon of blue sky to the open sea. By now there were some quite strong gusts building and *Huffler's* rigging hummed in tune, thus ending a wonderful day's gentle creek-crawling in exhilarating fashion.

After a busy day creek-crawling in and out of the Blackwater's many creeks and ditches, Huffler *settles for the night, at the very top of Goldhanger Creek.*

The Glorious Creek

The atmosphere just like a theatre,
my seat the cosy cabin of the tiny pocket ship,
sat silently in her mud print while all around the merry dance
of the day's end being played out once more.
The audible sounds of mother nature at her very best echo all
about in the stillness of the darkening light,
the night sky still tinged with blues and reds.
While beneath me the bubbling and gurgling sound, playing
like sweet music from the awakening soft mud,
as a retreating tide trickles gently away towards the main.
The chattering of oystercatchers feasting on an evening meal,
as tiny sandhoppers jump for joy in their hundreds, where
mud gives way to an inlet of golden sand.
Distant flickering of navigation buoys pulse hypnotically,
like a heartbeat of the night, the half-moon's glow gently
shimmering on the wet muddy surface of the creek bed,
as sweet fusion of salty aromas fill the now still air.
For this is the magic hour of The Glorious Creek.

Tony Smith - Summer 2010

88

Chapter Nine
Goldhanger Creek

Goldhanger Creek at half tide. This image shows the two mooring posts once visible at the creek mouth, originally erected by local farmers more than 100 years ago for smacks and barges to moor against, but today both posts have disappeared.

THE lower creek is visible at half tide or before on the main river. It has oyster layings that are still worked on its northern edges from Gore Saltings, along Bulham beach and its solitary hut up to Joyce's Creek. The layings create a hazard for craft of deeper draft, but a small boat can safely sail along this shore exploring and soaking in the scenery, which is a real treat if on the north side of the river around high water. The Ordnance Survey map of 1805 shows the creek used to reach up to the bottom of Fish Street where the days catch would have been unloaded from a smack at the quay and taken up to the village square. Here The Chequers Inn which dates back to the 15th century and remains relatively unchanged serves some of the finest real ales and home cooked food on this side of the river. Today stone-clad seawalls line both banks of the creeks relatively short and straight upper reach offering as you approach, pretty views of St Peter's Church tower above the trees. At high tide there is between 3 and 6 feet of water at the head of the creek which has been dammed to reclaim land that is now used as a playing field. Spritsail barges once landed at the creek's adjacent fields, while fishing smacks would have off-loaded their cargo into a pit on the corner of the western seaward end which, known locally as Fishpits Corner.

The hulk Snowdrop *is a dominant feature inside the creek*

Five-fingered starfish would have been stored in the pit for spreading as a fertiliser on the surrounding fields. Barges still use the outer creek today for drying out on its relatively flat surface, though incredibly in 2010 the two mooring posts, positioned more than a century ago, succumbed to the ravages of the sea and over enthusiastic boats and have been demolished. The eastern side of the creek mouth has some small shingle and sand beaches, the outer one called 'The Shoe' they all make decent dinghy landing. Just off the beach the hulk of 'stackie' barge *Snowdrop* sits entangled with sea weed, but as the tide gently rises in the creek her bulk covers, leaving her rudder post standing proud above the surface. I have seen pictures of *Snowdrop* in her heyday under sail. Built in Harwich in 1879 she was last used as a timber lighter at Heybridge, but like hundreds of other Thames barges on the East Coast, she has ended up as old decaying bones inhabiting their final birth in a quiet creek. Opposite, the

The oyster beds in Goldhanger Creek are owned by Maldon Oyster & Seafood Company, who not only produce Native oysters but are one of the largest producers of Pacific oysters. The oysters here are farmed in a line of trestles that reach from the lower end of the creek up to Joyce's Creek. Locals use the moored fishing boat as a bearing to keep clear of the cages but yellow marker buoys are positioned at the outer limits of the fishery.

small wooden slipway is owned and maintained by the Goldhanger Sailing Club, whose delightful little clubhouse and grounds sit just over the seawall next to the Essex jam-makers Wilkin and Sons organic fruit fields. It is widely known that the Bentall name is associated with a famous yacht called Jullanor, but it was working the nearby fields in the 18th century that yeoman farmer William Bentall invented the famous Bentall's Goldhanger plough. The plough was a revolution at the time and was in demand from farmers near and far. To cope with demand a larger site was found in nearby Heybridge where the company went on to become a large successful agricultural machinery makers and one of the biggest employers in the area. William's son Edward later took over the business and in 1839 the name changed to E H Bentall and Co. The Bentalls even went on to develop their own car; 100 were built at the Heybridge factory and in 1907 an advertisement showed three models available priced at £220, £240 and £305.

The neighbouring Joyce's Creek can be found just east of Goldhanger. The creek has a scattering of small beaches which are a delight to visit on a summer's day. The largest beach an extending spit of shingle that reaches eastward from its western side. This is a good place to beach the boat or drop anchor just inside it where islands of saltmarsh can be found. Barges once came in here to dock at the nearby farm at the head of the creek. In summer contented lambs can be seen roaming the seawalls and Joyce's marshes. Goldhanger's other neighbouring creek is just up river past Bound's Farm Island which is a saline tolerant oasis.

Anchored inside Joyce's Creek. The beautiful spit is also a fine beach for swimming.

Bound's Farm Island. At high tide the lower lying saltmarsh is covered creating the saline tolerant island, ideal for exploring and poling about in a dinghy. The withies mark an old farm hard where barges would once bring up. Many cobble stones of the hard are still discernable today at low water.

Wilkin's Creek, also known as Wager's Creek borders Gardener's Farm and Bound's Farm, the latter from where fruity organic aromas waft over the seawall during the summer growing season. Like Joyce's, there are saltings that can be navigated near to high tide. Farm fields and marshland beside these creeks contains red hills, and an abundance of wild birds. The creeks are also full of mud which is consummate for drying out in for a quiet night.

Experience the ambience of Wilkin's Creek, another Creeksailor favourite. Lots of soft mud, many stumps, islands of saltmarsh and a red hill set in the 'cant'. The very head of the creek has a small rusting iron bridge, and the saltings here are used by wildfowlers during the winter.

*"The invading Vikings of 991 are reputed to have
entered the island through this very creek"*

Chapter Ten
Northey Island, Southey, Limbourne and Awl Creeks

ON A RISING tide it is well worth sailing passed Mundon Stone Point keeping to this southern shoreline and head towards Northey Island and Maldon. Meander among the saltings at Cooper's Creek where, on one side, there are superb views of the grand Osea manor house, and on the other, Stansgate Abbey Farm, both notable landmarks.

Taking the Southey Creek route up along this peaceful shoreline towards Maldon is not the chosen route for the majority. This area dries around two hours either side of high water, but offers a rewarding sail to those who venture up there.

*Southey Creek, facing south-east from the very top of the creek. Shallow and wide creeks such as
Southey and Limbourne provide a relatively flat surface area to dry out on.*

The shoreline along here is dotted with saltmarsh which is cut into by small rills making it ideal for exploring.

Limbourne Creek is an ideal place to dry out if you are looking for a relaxing night aboard. Like Goldhanger and many others, the creek has been dammed to either reclaim land for farming or prevent flooding, and you can easily clamber up on the seawall for a scout around. The seawall dam has reduced the length of the creek considerably, but it is an idyllic spot, and wide enough to turn full circle if coming in under sail.

The view from the seawall of inner Limbourne Creek, now an inland oasis.

The top of the wall is also a good vantage point to study the inner creek which is now a freshwater haven for species such as the reed warbler. You can also see the old canal which was dug out from the creek mouth in the 1830s. It is just over a mile long and was used by lighters delivering coal to the nearby farm. Further along at the top of Southey Creek is the 'Stakes' an ancient causeway crossing to Northey Island, which is approximately 3 feet high in places, so it is best to time your crossing as near to high water as possible. As well as being a remote and perfect haven for wildlife, Northey Island is linked to the famous Battle of Maldon in 991 AD. The island is where the Viking invaders were thought to have stopped on a rising tide and made camp until low water before making their assault on the town, which forms the inspiration for the dramatic poem about local hero Bryhtnoth (pronounced Brithnoth).

It was on August 10 that the Essex Army, commanded by Bryhtnoth, put up a brave fight in a vain attempt to defend their town. Alas, just when the Saxons were in sight of victory, Bryhtnoth was slain, the Danes

Low water in Limbourne Creek. The creek ends abruptly at the seawall dam.

Northey Island. Owned and managed by The National Trust.

took Maldon and later set up camp at Danbury.

Standing on the causeway today you can almost feel the presence of those invading Vikings charging across the mudflats, marshes and fields. In recognition of his bravery, in 2006 a 9 ft bronze statue of Bryhtnoth, designed by local sculptor John Doubleday, was erected at the end of the promenade. There are no facilities for landing boats on Northey Island and visits on foot have to be booked in advance with the National Trust who became its owners in 1978. It is now an important bird sanctuary and worth a visit. Recently I stayed the night on *Huffler* in Limbourne Creek, having pre-booked a visit to Northey Island, which is just a short walk along the seawall. From the land side of the causeway it is about a half-an-hour walk to the warden's cottage where you need to check in.

Looking back across the 'Stakes' from Northey Island. Invading Vikings are thought to have charged across this causeway and battled in the nearby fields.

Symbols of East Coast seafaring. The two rudders of sailing barge hulks Gillman *and* Mistley *on Northey Island.*

The decaying hulk of Mistley *sits on the saltings beside Awl Creek, Northey Island.*

The only other house on the island was built by the islands former owner Sir Norman Angel, a writer and Nobel Peace Prize winner. This unusual building has a tower like structure which contains a master bedroom at the top offering stunning views across the estuary.

Visiting by foot means you are able to walk around the gardens and take a look at Sir Norman Angel's folly, which he built after WW2. The unique little arches that span the opening of the folly are formed with reclaimed church stones.

Visitors can also take a walk on the marshes and have a good look over the hulks of two spritsail sailing barges, *Mistley* and *Gillman.* Much of *Mistely's* superstructure is still there and the sight of the two rudders still standing up proudly out of the saltmarsh is quite impressive.

Since 1997 *Mistley* has been the subject of an adopt a wreck scheme.

The scheme is run by the Nautical Archaeology Society, who's aim is to preserve our archaeological heritage. Her slowly decaying structure is being meticulously recorded on an annual basis by members of the London Maritime Archaeology Group, which has adopted her.

The complex system of creeks and ditches that make up the greater part of the island today were run dry during the 18th century when land was reclaimed by the building of a seawall. Now though, there are a few areas where you can enter as the seawall has been breached as part of the coastal realignment. The constricted and vein like Awl Creek, which winds into the marshes, can be entered north-west of the island before it eventually runs parallel to the seawall along Collier's Reach where some erosion is noticeable. There is a lot of mud but it is navigable and in a small boat you can get right up to *Mistley's* remains.

The invading Vikings of 991 are reputed to have entered the island through this very creek.

Awl Creek is part of a complex system of tidal ditches that flood, covering Northey Island's saltmarsh at high spring tides.

The ornate folly on Northey Island.

*"A place where salt water swirls in crab holes
and gurgles at the movement of the tide"*

Chapter Eleven
St Lawrence Bay Ditches

ALONG the southern side of the river, in the sweeping panorama of St Lawrence Bay, the deep water contour of the main channel is lined with withies. From these withies to the shoreline just over half-a-mile away the murky waters cover tidal mudflats.

Fortunately, a small boat is able to venture into the creeks and ditches that emerge from the ebbing tide. There are seven creeks and ditches, among them St Lawrence Creek and the two Transit Creeks. These creeks and ditches traverse two miles of mudflats that reach eastward from The Stone to Pewet Island, Bradwell. This is a place where salt water swirls in crab holes and gurgles at the movement of the tide as it trickles along the smaller rills and gutways that cut through the putty-looking clay. On a summer's day all around the smooth surfaces glisten in the sunshine. At the joining of mud and shoreline, green ascending fields roll towards a wide eastern sky, an image in complete contrast to the lunar-like landscape below at low water.

This hidden muddy world is also a nutrient-rich feeding ground for waders such as redshank and sanderling, oystercatcher and dunlin, which can often be seen sifting the mud for the abundance of invertebrate that dwell below its slippery surface. This is a very special place on the river for the work-weary small-boat sailor, and a welcome respite from the rigours of the modern world.

The two Transit Creeks, and the ditches below, do become very narrow as you make your way along them, so if you are taking a cruiser in there

The gateway to a muddy world, the transit markers at St Lawrence Bay.

the likelihood is that you may just get stuck fast, or find it difficult getting out again. This may well be intentional, for if you are looking for solitude you will rarely see another boat here.

The smaller dinghy however, will be able to venture deeper in for about a quarter-of-a-mile and still get out again.

St Lawrence Creek has a wider entrance of around 75 feet and is navigable at half-tide. A favourable south easterly wind allows a short beat, southwards into the creek where at the turn you are able to take the south west fork for a short distance before it peters out into a trickle. Or take the lovely reach east all the way to Bradwell Creek, invariably a blissful journey.

For the avid creek and ditch-crawler it is particularly rewarding visiting the area on a neap tide when an hour after low tide there is about 3 foot of water. Around this time there is just enough of the briny stuff to navigate among the moon-like dunes. At the junction with St Lawrence Creek and Bradwell Creek there is a thick wooden stump hazard sticking up about 2 feet which is visible at that time.

St Lawrence Creek, an hour before low water. Viewed facing west. Over the mudflats on the right of this picture is the main river, to the left is Beacon Hill.

I have played around in here on an ebb tide and grounded for 45 minutes near the bottom of low water, a time when only mast tops are visible out

Transit Creek. Polling about the muddy ditches in the dinghy.

on the main river. My excuse: it was about time to anchor for a cuppa! Across the mud from here is Orplands where the seawall has been breached as part of the coastal realignment.

From the depths of Transit Creek, West Mersea can just be made out to the right of this image.

About halfway along in St Lawrence Creek there is also the taller and somewhat lonesome withie marker. It stands in the creek roughly midway on the south side. This is no ordinary withie as it has been added to with what appears to be a metal pole. But this only becomes a potential hazard when the creek and ditches are covered (update 11/2011 hazard earmarked for removal). There is a small beach inland along this stretch for which this marker could well have been placed. At an area of saltmarsh above here is the high water limit of the creek from where it is possible to reach a little further into the saltings.

Transit Creek is above St Lawrence Creek and has the rusting transit markers near its mouth. The transit markers strike a line across the river, which is the western boundary of the Tollesbury and Mersea Native Oyster Fishery Ltd. Transit Creek is another small waterway that winds its way into the mudflats, as you go further in you notice that its width decreases to 8 feet, where it is more accurately described as a ditch. It eventually forks south-west towards Ramsey Island before disappearing into the mud. Further inland is a small beach and a private slipway, which can be reached nearer high water. These creeks give the adventurer a lot of fun in a dinghy, either under sail or with an oar when in about 2 foot of water. The mud here is very deep so it is not wise to venture out of the boat. Beacon Hill rises above the creeks and was once used by smugglers to warn inland villages of Customs ships coming up-river. The remaining ditches below St Lawrence Creek are all similar to the Transit Creeks but are silted at the entrances, though they do retain some water inside and are just navigable in a dinghy.

The offending stump at the junction of St Lawrence Creek and Bradwell Creek. This image was taken at low water neaps when there is about a foot of water here.

"Anything island-like has a magnet pull
on Huffler's anchor"

Chapter Twelve
Shoals

THE Thirslet Spit in all its glory: an artwork of mother nature, right here slap-bang in the middle of the River Blackwater. Sadly, like the other shoals, and understandably for obvious reasons, it is avoided like the plague by the majority of yachtsmen because larger yachts often get neaped here. Even so, most of my sailing on the river involves navigating around it, and sometimes even over it. Whatever your fancy, it pays to get to know this beautiful shoal up close, the geography of which unfolds before you in layer upon layer of cockle, oyster, winkle, and mussel shells. From full shells at the very top, graduating in size to broken shells. Then finer shells, until right at the water's edge, there is fine sand. The end result of endless tide erosion. Who knows how many thousands of years it has taken to reach this pure form?

Thirslet Spit snares another yacht. To be neaped on a spit like Thirslet is a nightmare scenario for many yachtsmen.

Where shoals like the Thirslet Spit is concerned, the river can be likened to a flower in the sunlight its petals unfold to reveal the real beauty hidden beneath them, only in the case of this river it is the ebb of the tide.

The spit is another of the river's gems I enjoy visiting. Anything island-like has a magnet pull on *Huffler's* anchor. As long as your timing is right you couldn't want for a better anchorage for swimming and beachcombing. The spit is vast, a kind of horseshoe in shape with the creek to the north and an inner lagoon at low water springs.

At low water the spit also provides respite for the pocket cruiser in mid-river as in the lee of the spit, shelter can be found from strong winds in almost any direction.

An incredible amount of Harwich Harbour shingle has been placed at Shinglehead. This image gives us a good idea of the sheer volume of tidal water that flows in and out of the river twice a day.

Shinglehead Point: Thousands of tons of Harwich Harbour shingle have been pumped onto the foreshore here by maintenance dredgers, creating a man-made island. It is hoped that this experimental sea defence measure will help prevent further erosion of the nearby saltmarsh. Since taking the above photograph restricted landing signs have been erected on this island of shingle by Essex Wildlife Trust. Protected species of wild birds are now nesting on the shingle. The signs advise not to land from the end of April until the end of July, which is the birds breeding season. If you have to land during this period, there are two green marks, between which is the preferred area to land.

The mudflats of the Nass reach far out towards Mersea from here and are a favourite for winkle picking at low tide. There is also an ancient fish trap dating from 600 to 1000BC that can be seen at low water springs. When coming from the north of the river, across from Bradwell into Tollesbury, or heading up to Old Hall, I have often managed to cut across the Nass, keeping close to the shingle; hopping over a couple of hours either side of high water and straight into the South Channel.

The south-western side of Thirslet Spit forms a lagoon of water inside the shoal. Bradwell can be seen to the east.

From Mill Point there are half a dozen smaller shell shoals to avoid scraping over until you meet this huge shoal that extends out from the shoreline at the eastern side of the entrance to Mell Creek, almost parallel to the old Tollesbury pier. This is another shingle shell shoal and on an ebb tide it guides the murkier water from the muddy bottom of Mell Creek into the main river. This creates an aquarium-like pocket of water behind it, where it's always nice to anchor for a quiet swim.

The spit at Mell Creek extends far out into the river, providing either a good landing spot or clear water to anchor for a swim.

Chapter Thirteen
A Creeksailor's Tool Kit

CREEK sailing can sometimes be a very fickle pastime. Without doubt reaching the top of a winding inland creek which perhaps courses through some breath-taking scenery, is an uplifting experience. Many of the gentler and more pleasant meanderings are hard-earned rewards for the avid ditch and creek crawler able to adapt at a moment's notice as situations unfold; maybe taking an unintended route that later pays off with a previously undiscovered waterway, or a place to stop for the night. Each creek presents a different challenge and so it pays to have a few bits of kit that may come in handy for the job in hand.

One example is Cooper's Creek, which becomes so narrow that in its final stages it is no longer navigable under sail. On occasions such as this I try to use a canoe paddle, an oar, or Norfolk Broad-style quant pole to help propel myself the remaining distance. I find the paddle works in deeper holes, and stows easily in the cabin or dinghy when not needed. But if you have room a quant pole is invaluable. More often than not all your seamanship skills will be called on when it comes to creek sailing. If you sail a cutter-rigged craft like I do you will become even more adept, for there are times when it can become a bit of a circus act: juggling spinning plates on top of sticks.

Basic tool kit. Note the all-important kettle.

A shallow draft boat is desirable, and my particular preference is a lifting rudder and centre plate, both of which will frequently be scraping the bottom, though at least they can be raised quickly. Although not essential, I recently fitted *Huffler* with an echo-sounder, which I find a useful aid in deeper water. I also keep a sharp eye out while standing up at the tiller, for when conditions are calm you can generally see the bottom. The sounding-pole is simply a 6-8 feet length of bamboo cane, but virtually any convenient length will do. I prefer the direct contact the sounding-pole gives you with the creek bed for judging your next move. As I sail mostly single-handed every control line on *Huffler* is ready to hand in the cockpit. They comprise four sheets for the headsails, plus two furling lines and one mainsheet.

Then there is one centre-plate and two rudder uphauls, two main halyards, two headsail halyards a topping lift. Oh, and on top of all that, there is the mooring line and the self-steering line. It all adds up to a lot of lines, so it is vital that you keep a tidy cockpit.

All too often when you enter your chosen creek the wind will be straight on the nose. This is where the juggling act begins as my better half's frequent concept of a multi-tasking male becomes a reality. With one hand on the tiller the other controls the sheets as well as the sounding pole, the plate has started to scrape so that has to be raised, too?

Undoubtedly, through trial and error, you will find a system that works for you. When beating into a narrow stretch of creek I often place a cushion on the cockpit floor where I can kneel and still have both hands on the sheets while controlling the helm with my hips.

However, there are times when *Huffler's* tiny staysail has taken us all the way in or back out of a creek.

The anchor is another item that gets constant use on board the pocket cruiser. The basic rules of good seamanship apply, so having one that is heavy enough to hold you in a tidal stretch of river will be ample for the upper pond-like reaches of a creek. On a day's creek-crawling the anchor might be used four or five times, possibly more so expect to be busy. Like many other cruiser sailors I adapt my boats for single-handed sailing. Working out a system that suits you and your boat, taking time in making any adjustments will in the end prove invaluable and will make the job of anchoring an enjoyable experience.

I am sure too many people never bother to stop anywhere where there isn't a floating mooring because they feel that getting out the anchor is a hassle. A smaller kedge anchor is also useful too. With the bow anchor set, I often use a small folding grapnel from *Huffler's* stern to position her for drying in a good position to guarantee a sound night's sleep.

It is true that things can get rather muddy at times, but one just gets used to it. It is a good idea to carry a couple of sponges to clean the anchor and deck. A small compass, a map or chart, a pair of sea-boots and binoculars round off the basic essentials.

I like to think I am a bit of a purist, endeavouring for the most part to sail or row, but I will not hesitate to use the small outboard motor that hangs on *Huffler's* transom, if it becomes necessary. After all, this is supposed to be a leisurely pastime. I also carry a couple of flares and a handheld VHF radio, a small handheld GPS unit is also useful, especially for retracing your tracks

My pocket cruiser is a Shipmate Senior class hull, which handles like a dinghy. It has a very shallow draught, just 11.5 inches, but has the added benefits of a lifting centre plate and rudder. As a convert to the traditional local working boats, I changed the original bermudan rig, creating a gaff-gutter rig. The end result is a small pocket yacht that suits the type of ditch-and-creek crawling I love to do on the river. Another boat I have cruised extensively inside the Blackwater is the robust 14 foot 9 inch Drascombe Scaffie with a 1 foot 3 inch draft and a simple lugsail rig. She was an ideal ditch-crawler and, with an adapted tent, made for good overnight camping. The Scaffie has the advantage that it is easy to trail behind a car, will fit into the smallest of garages, and can be safely left on a mooring. In 2009 I spent five consecutive nights on board my Scaffie cruising over 100 miles in and out of the Blackwater creeks. There is no centre plate to raise or lower and with two small bilge keels, and just one sheet to deal with, it is sailing at its most simplest.

Huffler is 16 foot 3 inches long and with her traditional gaff rig and small but cosy cabin, is an ideal pocket cruiser for the Blackwater.

Overnight camping on board the Scaffie dinghy while cruising on the River Blackwater.

This photogragh was taken at Brick House Farm dock in Lawling Creek while on a three-day cruise in Shoal Waters. Her accommodation is very similar in proportion to the Shipmate, but her handling is altogether different. She has a stiffer feel, being a much heavier boat and she tacks gracefully along the creeks. For my convenience, I have added one of those great British traditions, a Seagull auxiliary outboard.

Since writing this book Charles Stock has had to retire from sailing due to ill health. I am privileged to be able to say that in February 2011 I became the new owner of the 16 foot 6 inches long wooden gaff-cutter *Shoal Waters*. She has a creek sailing pedigree second to none, and I am already beginning to take her cruising to all the places mentioned in this book, as well her old haunts in the wider Thames Estuary.

*"Men would often spend hours lying cramped in the punt
in freezing conditions without firing a single shot"*

Chapter Fourteen
The Gun Punt

IT WAS during the winter months a century or so ago that wildfowling
from a gun punt was a common activity undertaken by fishermen,
bargemen and hunters. The gun punt, or duck punt as it is called by many
folk is a 15-22 feet long sturdy canoe like boat with a near flat bottom
and a beam measuring roughly 3 feet. Gun punts are of differing designs
and in those days could be commissioned from most of the boatbuilders
on the river, although it was not unusual for a fisherman to build his own.
Some resembled a large kayak and were fitted with a deck and coamings.
Others, like the Mersea-type punt, were generally open and canoe-like
with a single thwart, where a gun barrel up to 1.25 inches and 9 feet in
length could be secured by a heavy rope. The punt is usually painted in a
light grey colour for camouflage. The punter lies prone inside the boat
and paddles inconspicuously towards his prey. With the punt pointing
towards the birds a knock on the side of the punt was made to startle them
into flight, whereupon the shot was released with a huge 'boom'. More
often than not these men would set off in their duck punts on cold, foggy
mornings, or under cover of a late evening mist. It was a hard way to earn
a living or to provide food to put on to the table. Men would often spend
hours lying cramped in the punt in freezing conditions without firing a
single shot, returning home cold and empty-handed. It was also a
dangerous occupation as there were no such aids as a life-jacket, and the
punts had no buoyancy. There was also the threat of disappearing in the
deep mud if you were parted from the punt. These small vessels would
only ever be rowed by hand, or sailed, but they enabled the punter to pole
about in the saltings on a high tide or to search out the shallow tide lines
of the mudflats at low water. On a slightly larger scale, some farms used

decoy ponds dug on land adjacent to the river. Some of these are still visible at places such as the marshes beside Old Mill Creek and from the east bank of Gore Saltings at the head of Thirslet Creek. These ponds were used with an elaborate system of screens and nets to entice wintering wildfowl such as brent geese, dunlin, widgeon, teal and mallard. They were expensive to build, but with such a demand to supply the London markets with food, the high building costs could often be recouped in a couple of seasons. The use of the decoys ceased around 1900 but the punts continued with even larger guns until its decline in the fifties. The ancient tradition of punt-gunning is kept alive on the river today by one or two wildfowlers, and punts can still be seen moored in the saltings. There is a classic example of a Mersea gun punt, built by William Wyatt in 1919, which can be seen on display at the Mersea Museum. One man who has had a long connection with the boat is retired Mersea shipwright John Milgate. Now in his 80s, John was born on the waterside in one of the small cottages in the 'Old City.' He remembers his father would cycle down to East Mersea to go winkling, or sometimes see him unloading coal from a barge on the hard. John worked at the nearby Wyatt's yard learning his trade under the tutelage of William Wyatt, or the 'Admiral', as he was known. At this time in the 1940s gun punts were still being built for wildfowlers at Wyatt's shed which is where today's Dabchicks Sailing Club is built. A white painted sign on the shed read 'Punts For Sale' and an area to the left of the shed was known as 'Punt Bay' as many punts were kept on the foreshore. John remembers helping Bill Wyatt to build one of his last Mersea punts and the very last one produced by the yard was a special 12 foot version for a cousin of his, who wanted one for winkling. A simple white cotton sail could also be set from a punt and John has a picture from 1913 showing punts being raced by their owners.

They were useful boats; even when working on a yacht at the yard a punt would often be used as a steady work platform. Wyatt's built punts in clinker style with standard 3/8 inch thick planks for the topsides and the bottoms were made with 7 3/4 inch x ¾ inch pine boards. John said, "Bill had a wooden beam of 9 inch x 3 inch thick timber that he used as a jig to make the fore and aft curve in the bottom. He laid the pre-assembled bottom planks over it and propped them from the ceiling with other pieces of timber to hold the shape. I remember the boards were fastened with thick galvanised nails that had a better grip." John worked on a variety of boats during his working life, including yachts, smacks, brigs and bumkins. He also worked on many of the houseboats that today lay in the saltings beside Coast Road to Hove Creek. Having a life-long affection for the duck punt John used the Wyatt punt as a yardstick to build his own version of it. "It was about 2000 when I made the first one. It was not only intended for wildfowling but for pottering about or to race in as they are lovely little boats". The John Milgate version of a Wyatt punt can be built with just three sheets of 9 mm plywood, along with some strips of standard sized planed softwood, one or two other small pieces of timber, a box of screws and a pot of glue. Anyone with average woodworking skills should have no real problem building it. At just under 16 foot, it follows the traditional lines of the Wyatt punts. The punt has some particularly nice curves and has a small flare in the stern which was intended to give a bit more lift when in more of a sea. The open Mersea punts were intended for practical use in suitable weather conditions, so their seaworthiness was sometimes compromised, for it is not designed to be used in choppy waves. John's Mersea punt has the added benefit that being just under 16 feet in length it will fit into a standard car garage. One of the other features is that it can be sailed with an easily obtainable Optimist dinghy rig. The punts have no keel and are steered with a small oar held over the leeward side against a pin. Although flat bottomed there is around a 2.5 inch curve fore and aft from about two-thirds from the bow, but without any 'knuckle'. John is now fondly known as the 'Punt Father' by a small but growing number of enthusiasts. There are at present around 20 or so of these modern-day punters who, while no longer hunting wildfowl, enjoy cruising in them to places like 'Punt Alley', which is a top-of-tide creek through the saltings opposite West Mersea Yacht Club that takes you into Salcott Creek. During the winter there is also some friendly racing, too.

'Marsh Duck', *a John Milgate/Wyatt Mersea gun punt. Hand built by the author (under guidance) at John Milgate's boatshed.*

*"Works of canvas art, full of intricate details such as
hand-stitched eyes and hemp luff rope"*

Chapter Fifteen
Traditional Sailmaking

JUST A stone's throw from the top of Woodrolfe Creek, sitting on a
wooden bench behind the wonderfully textured Essex boarded exterior of
his workplace, sailmaker Steve Hall, of North Sea Sails, continues to ply
his trade in the time-proven ways dating back generations.

Steve makes, or what I would more accurately say creates, works of
canvas art full of intricate details such as hand stitched eyes and hemp
luff rope, with fine leather corner edging all sewn in by hand, the quality
of which is likely to last the lucky owner years of service.

It's almost a crime to have to use these sails, so complex is the fine
workmanship, but they are made to do a task and they do it superbly.
Steve's work can be seen on traditional sailing craft across the country,
and abroad, even as far away as the USA. But he also takes on small
repairs or adjustments for all manner of boats, from small gaff or lugsail
dinghies to huge East-Coast Thames barges, all in his cosy Aladdin's
Cave of a sail loft. His tools of the trade are simple enough; a sharp pair
of scissors, needles, one or two fids, a small mallet and, of course, the
sailmaker's leather palm.

There is also a few sewing machines in regular use, one of them a
straight-stitch Singer on which sailmaker Gayle Heard learnt to sew on.

Over the years a variety of materials have been used to make sails but generally the chosen cloth was cotton, until the early 1950s when Gowens of Mersea, who at the time had a loft in Tollesbury, made the first-ever terylene sail.

Watching Steve work a new canvas mains'l for a bumkin, while sitting on his bench is an image that is not often seen today. Many people might not even know that such a sailmaker exists here because Steve rarely advertises his services, preferring the age-old "word-of-mouth" option. There is no fancy office here, not even an answer-phone. Steve prefers his trusty old ring dial-up telephone, another hint of his traditional ethos. He is also known locally as the master sailmaker, and having looked at his workmanship it is a title he thoroughly deserves. I have called on Steve to make a variety of sails for various small boats and he usually asks to bring him a scaled drawing of the proposed sail plan. Steve has a good look over the drawing and after a little tweaking of dimensions (if

Steve Hall of North Sea Sails, working the canvas.

needed) confirms that it will be fine. Before entering the upstairs area of the sail loft I put on two pairs of woolly socks, as no shoes are allowed up on the loft's boarded floor. While Steve sat at his bench hand-stitching a luff reefing cringle eye we chatted, and he told me how his good friend and author, the late John Leather, visited most Fridays to talk about boats.

The sailmaker's tools.

While I watched him work the thick needle through the sail cloth with his well-worn leather palm, I asked: "Surely that needle must occasionally have come through the leather and into your hand?" "Yes," he replied with a smile, "once or twice."

Among numerous old marine bits and pieces hanging from the rafters in the loft was a huge elm dead eye, measuring roughly 8 inches in diameter and 4 inches thick. It was given to him by a local fisherman, who picked it up in his nets while in the North Sea. One can only wonder how old it is and what happened to the rest of the vessel?

Chapter Sixteen
Traditional Boatbuilding

FROM the water's edge work can often be seen in progress at boat yards up and down the river. At Maldon, shipwrights can be found in yards such as the Downes Road Boatyard or at Shipways Yard where Adrian Riva is based. Lower down there is Ian Danskin at Cooks Yard and on the water front Jim Maynard can be found.

Across the water in Heybridge James Byam Shaw makes spars, and if you sail up Lawling Creek to the Blackwater Marina at Maylandsea you can usually see a barge in dry dock undergoing restoration works.

Walk along the hard at Tollesbury and you will probably see traditional skills being used by men like shipwright Paul Drake and at West Mersea there are shipwrights such as David Mills, as well as Peter Clarke's Boatyard. This concentrated nucleus of skills should mean a bright future not only for the traditional local boats but in preserving our national marine heritage.

I had the pleasure of meeting Maldon shipwright David Patient out on the river where he was doing some minor repairs to the Thames sailing barge *Phoenician*, which was dried out on a flat hard lower down-river at Goldhanger, something barge skippers have been doing for more than a 100 years.

I was able to help her owner, Grant Littler with scrubbing below her waterline. She was built in 1922 and at 84 feet long giving her a scrub is not a task taken lightly. Fortunately, she was in pretty good condition with no sign of weed or barnacles, just a slight film of mud from her Maldon mud berth. When barges used tar as an anti-foul, they would dry out here, then the crew would sometimes light fires beside the hull to melt the tar, making it easier to scrape. I take my hat off to today's owners of these handsome craft, for this is a labour of love that is both on-going and expensive.

Phoenician *dried out just off an area called The Shoe at Goldhanger Creek.*

Shipwright David Patient forming a huge spar out of a solid piece of larch.

I also met David at his Fullbridge yard where he was in the process of rebuilding the fishing smack *Varuna*. It was an incredible sight, as was the huge spar he was making for another fishing smack, *Excelsior*, out of a huge piece of solid timber, possibly one of the largest pieces of larch to be used for boatbuilding around these shores for decades.

At the other end of the river, around the top of the Strood at West Mersea, and a short walk into the village of Peldon, the skills used in traditional boatbuilding are also quietly under way. Peldon is linked with boatbuilding on the Blackwater and Gerard Swift, of Swift Boats, is continuing this tradition at his well-equipped boatyard here.

The last time I was there was to accompany a friend to look at an original clinker dinghy, which was being restored to its former glory. Speaking to Gerard about the type of boats that come into his yard, he pointed out a typical example, a winkle brig, which is one of the seven remaining original brigs of approximately 30 boats that once worked on the river under sail. The winkle brig would have been used for oyster-dredging as well as winkling.

Gerard continues to maintain this wonderful boat for her owner, who races her at classic boat events on the river. Watching him working some new oak ribs into a lugsail dinghy's clinker hull was fascinating. After half-an-hour spent in the steam box, the solid strips of green oak become plyable and are moulded into the hull shape and clenched with copper nails. Gerard was originally based in Maldon where his father owned Cook's Yard. "My father purchased the yard from Cliff Cook, who was the son of Walter Cook. We had 16 years there," he told me.

Gerard also spent time there as barge mate on *Reminder* and his father owned barge *Dawn*. The *Dawn* was built in 1897 at Maldon for the stack trade and has since had a very interesting history that includes a major restoration project undertaken by the *Dawn* Trust at Heybridge where she was relaunched in May 2007.

A 12 foot long 1954 Sea Ranger *in the process of having some new ribs and planking fitted.*

A variety of boats in one of the Swift Boats workshops, Peldon.

Chapter Seventeen
Small-Boat Sailors

NO BOOK about the small-boat sailor on the River Blackwater would be complete without a mention of Charles Stock. For all boating enthusiasts, Charlie has become a local legend following his countless adventures all over the Thames Estuary in his pocket cruiser *Shoal Waters*, during which time he has clocked up over 75,000 nautical miles, every inch without an engine. Unless away on one of his expeditions, Charles' unmistakable 16 foot Fairey Falcon could nearly always be seen happily bobbing up and down on her mooring just up-river at Ballast Hole, Heybridge. Like others on the river, I have on many occasions spotted

Charles Stock on his mooring at Ballast Hole Heybridge.

Charles' distinctive green hull, often resplendant with red topsail, but in April 2009 I had the pleasure of sailing with him on *Shoal Waters* up to Maldon. Sadly, with health fading, that year turned out to be his last sailing single-handed in *Shoal Waters*, so I was delighted that he agreed for me to capture the trip on film. To mark his last year in sailing, and on behalf of the Blackwater Small-Boat Sailors Group, I organised a small-boat rendezvous with Charles at his mooring in Ballast Hole. The get-together was arranged at very short notice and six pocket cruisers attended, we all rafted alongside *Shoal Waters* for a cuppa and a natter. As a tribute to the prince of small-boat sailing, this is an interview I did with him at Blackwater Sailing Club in June 2010.

TS: Charles, there are so many things I would like to ask you but there is not enough time, so I will try and keep it as brief as I can, but firstly thanks for taking the time to do this question-and-answer interview. I'd like to start by asking you what was it that first made you want to get afloat in a small sailing boat?

CS: As a small boy we would go to Southend and get rides out on the beach boats where I would trail my hands in the water. This was one of the first memories that come to mind. Also, in the summer of 1947 on Gare Loch, in Scotland, while as a Royal Marine deck-hand on an LCA, I noticed a tremendous yacht fleet there, and also a German windfall yacht called *Orion*, plus a substantial fleet of naval 14 foot sailing dinghies. At first I did not realise how one might get on one of these until I discovered that there was no-one there to say yes or no. So I found the kit and took one out. No-one said anything, so from then on I had one out every spare moment for the rest of that summer.

TS: What was your most memorable trip afloat and why?

CS: As Watch Officer on the Sail Training Ship with an all-girl crew racing up the Irish Sea with a force 7 to 8 behind us and a little cockney girl from London beside me holding the wheel. They were terrible boats to keep straight, and I could hear her muttering under her breath, as she struggled with the wheel, "Trouble is no one will ever believe me."

TS: If you could have added anything in the way of modern gadgets to *Shoal Waters* what would it have been?

CS: Long pause. Well, we did not have any floorboards when we first started out, or a decent compass, but these were added later as and when extra money became available. There is nothing that I can think of that I would want now though.

TS: It is very clear to me that your enthusiasm for small-boat cruising is still as strong as ever. What is it that has kept you enthralled over the past 50 years or so?

CS: Well, just the sheer magic of it. The unlimited variations; no two trips are the same. And the vast number of places to visit within 50 miles or so of my sailing club.

TS: What is the most useful object on-board *Shoal Waters* that you keep close to hand?

CS: Two objects, really, the sounding pole, which is an 8 foot cane, and a pair of binoculars.

TS: Do you think a pair of binoculars are more useful than a GPS finder?

CS: Well, have you ever tried looking at a girl in a bikini through GPS? Chuckles.

TS: Cooking on board a small boat can be quite an art, what is your favourite meal when at anchor?

CS: The old Fray Bento's steak and kidney pudding.

TS: Cooked in the kettle, no doubt?

CS: Oh, yes. More chuckles.

TS: What is your favourite book?

CS: Riddle of the Sands.

TS: Is there anyone in particular whom you think may have influenced you in the kind of small-boat cruising that you do?

CS: Oh, yes, Francis B Cooke, who sailed from Fambridge in the 1880s and who died at the age of 100, some years ago now.

TS: With regards to books, fiction or non-fiction?

CS: Definitely non-fiction; I never knowingly read fiction.

TS: Here on the River Blackwater we are spoilt for choice as to where to drop the anchor. If you had to pick two places to anchor *Shoal Waters* where would that be?

CS: Inside Lawling Creek and up Ray Island.

TS: You have written many articles over the years that have appeared in yachting magazines and also a lovely book, 'Sailing Just For Fun', in which you described so many of your adventures. Is writing something you have always been interested in or something that has developed from your sailing adventures?

CS: Well, yes, I've always written things down, and I kept a diary when I was in the forces, which you were not supposed to do. But I had written of various experiences, most of which have not gone anywhere, but it certainly is nice to have written an article and seen it published.

TS: What is the most expensive item you have had to replace on *Shoal Waters?*

CS: It was the rudder. I broke it sailing on the Norfolk Broads when she failed to tack and I was driven astern into the bank.

TS: Have you ever cruised in company or rallied with other small boats?

CS: Yes, I was cruiser captain at this club for four or five years and organised the most successful cruises ever, including two separate trips through the Havengore Bridge.

TS: Charles I hope you don't mind me reminding you but you will be 83 in a couple of months, so can we still expect to see you cruising the East Coast in *Shoal Waters*?

CS: The first time I sailed out the river was 1949, and last year was my 60th year. I think that looks like being the end of my sailing career as the old body is starting to pack up now. But to crown everything, I was recently awarded the Royal Cruising Club's annual medal for services to cruising.

TS: It has been said that the Thames Estuary is one of the most difficult areas in the world to navigate a boat? Would you agree?

CS: Well, I don't know about the most difficult in the world as I have not sailed the rest of the world, for there are certain incredibly difficult places elsewhere. But it is a notorious area and it does produce a superb type of sailor.

TS: Do you have a favourite destination or passage that you like to make for?

CS: Well, the jewel in the crown must be the Butley River, which comes off the river Ore. Its in beautiful Suffolk countryside with a lovely watermill at the top, and on the way up the wonderful sight on rising ground the mass of sand martin's nesting.

TS: You are well-known for your single-handed sailing. Have you ever had a crew on *Shoal Waters*?

CS: Oh, yes, once our children were old enough to be left alone my wife Joy sailed with me for many years. She accompanied me on trips around the north Norfolk coast, down to the south coast, across to Dunkirk and Calais, and many inland routes on various canals. She was a superb crew. To give you an example, on the day of the trip to the Dunkirk anniversary, I anchored overnight in Pegwell Bay because Ramsgate was solid with boats. In the morning I had left it a shade late and the boat could not sail off. As we were still aground I called Joy, who was still asleep. She leaped out of her bunk in her nightie and jumped into the water, together we were able to move the boat into deeper water and sail off. There aren't many wives who would do that.

TS: You have sailed over 75,000 nautical miles in *Shoal Waters*, that is a lot of miles. Pleasure sailing in the UK is unregulated. Do you have any sailing qualifications?

CS: Laughs. Well, I have passed the written part of RYA Yachtmaster examination, but in fact, my wife Joy, is more qualified than me because she has taken the practical as well.

TS: Besides sailing on *Shoal Waters* and before that your half-decker, what other craft have you sailed?

CS: Well, I have done six trips as Watch Officer on Sail Training Schooners. In 1947 I sailed an 85-ton ketch from Glasgow to the Channel Isles and I've also taken part in numerous ocean races in the North Sea, as well as several East Coast EAORA races around the Thames Estuary. I've also taken part in the Coronation dinghy race around the Isle of Wight, which was a unique occasion.

TS: I'd like to say it has been a pleasure to speak to you again Charles, and thanks for giving me this interview. I would also like to thank you on behalf of all the small-boat sailors, who have enjoyed reading about your adventures and learning about how much fun there can be had afloat with minimal equipment and outlay.

CS: Righty-O Tony, and thank you, too.

More Small-Boat Sailors

Mike Newport of Goldhanger SC in his 19ft Cornish Shrimper, 'Swallow' and Antony Gambia of Stone SC in his 17ft Pirate Express 'Jakaba' make way to a small-boat sailor's rendezvous.
Mike has this to say about the Blackwater. "Get away from the main fairway on the right tide and weather, and you can find hidden places where very few others have ventured. You can spend a whole season (and more) exploring the north and south shores without having to leave the confines of the estuary. It may take you years to get the right conditions to visit some of these haunts, but once visited, especially if you have over-nighted amongst the marshlands and their wildlife, the memories will last for the rest of your life".

Small-boat sailor Brian Goodbourn can often be seen cruising the creeks of the River Blackwater in his 16 ft Winkle Brig, Patience.

Chapter Eighteen
Creeks Of The River Blackwater

SOME of the creeks in the river are high water creeks best explored a couple of hours around high tide. Others reveal themselves around half tide to low water which is a good time to explore them. Some are a mixture of the two. Local names of many creeks derive mainly from the old fishermen or wildfowlers who would name every patch of mud and puddle of water, having spent most of their lives working them. But one or two others have come about in more recent times by other groups that use the area.

The list is of 62 creeks that are known by a name and I have been able to navigate under sail or oar, some just. A few distinguishing features are also noted.

There are still a few small creeks in the river without names, and there is also the possibility other names may have been lost in the mists of time having once been used for one or two of the creeks already listed.

I am constantly seeking information that may lead to further identification of these creeks, therefore as my research continues this list will continue to be updated.

1. Abbotts Hall Creek: Top-of-tide, saltings, rebuilt barge dock, red hill.
2. Awl Creek: Leads into Northey Island, hulks, top-of-tide, birds.
3. Back Creek: Mudberths in saltings. High water, hulk.
4. Back Channel: Shallow high tide creek opposite Maldon Hythe, hulks.
5. Bawley Creek: High tide, Osea Island's natural harbour, saltings, wharf.
6. Besom Creek: Called Buzzen locally. All states, smack moorings and

fine beach, Cobmarsh Island.

7. Big Fleet Creek: Dammed, top-of-tide, saltings, Tollesbury Wick natural marshland. May have been known as Chalkie's and Marfleet.
8. Bontin's Creek: Around high water. Hard, saltings, road.
9. Bowles Creek: Saltings, around half tide. Many wooden remains along bank.
10. Bradwell Creek: Leads into the marina, barge wharf, Pewet Island, most states.
11. Bulham Creek: Also called Bullen. Top-of-tide, beach, saltmarsh. Has also been known as East Dreen.
12. Chatterson's Creek: Saltings, high tide.
13. Curlew Creek: High tide, hulk, torpedo boat wreck, saltings.
14. Collin's Creek Upper: Low tide, shingle, mudflats. Has two steel wrecks used as target practice by WW2 fighter planes.
15. Collin's Creek Lower: Low tide, shingle, mudflats. The Collin's Creeks also have ancient fish traps which run east to west for about a mile.
16. Cooper's Creek: A top-of-tide creek, saltings.
17. Death Creek: Also called Dead Man's Creek. High tide, saltings. Has links to 19th century smugglers.
18. Decoy Creek: High tide, saltings, two small wrecks and sluice gates.
19. Earl Creek: Mudflats, revealed around half-tide to low water.
20. Feldy Creek: Top-of-tide, saltmarsh. Also known as 'Punt Alley' when it becomes a top of tide 'way', into Little Ditch and Salcott Creek.
21. Ford Creek: Mudflats, main creek can be navigated around low water. Beside ancient roman causeway.
22. Goldhanger Creek: Mudflats. Oysters farmed by Maldon Oyster Co in lower creek, most states, top-of-tide into dammed upper creek, hulk.
23. Gunner's Creek: Top-of-tide, saltings and mudflats, ancient fort Othona, St Peter-on-the-Wall Chapel and Linnett's cottage.
24. Heybridge Creek: High tide creek. Urban, wharf, hulks, saltings.
25. Horseshoe Creek: Saltmarsh, top-of-tide, small wildfowlers creek.
26. Hove Creek: High tide, saltings, beach. St Peter's Meadow, can just

get in here in a dinghy.

27. Joyce's Creek: Saltings, beaches and marshes, large sand spit.
28. Joyce's Head Creek: Dammed, saltings.
29. Johnny's Creek: Near high tide, mud and saltmarshes.
30. Larnch Creek: Low water, mudflats. Leads off Ford Creek up to Decoy Creek.
31. Lawling Creek: Most states. Often has seals on western side. Marina and Brick House Farm dock.
32. Limbourne Creek: Dammed, a top-of-tide creek. Land borders National Trust, saltings, disused canal. Called Hazes Creek by fishermen and at one time called Lime Brook.
33. Little Ditch: Also known as Copt Hall Creek. From half-tide into Copt Hall, saltmarsh, countryside, red hill.
34. Mayland Creek: Saltings and countryside, top-of-tide to reach the barge docks.
35. Mundon Creek: Top-of-tide, saltings, wreck.
36. Mell Creek: Also known as Mill Creek, top-of-tide, marshes. Fine yachts have moored in here as well as some of Tollesbury's former fishing fleet of smacks. Beside former crab and winkle line.
37. Mersea Creek: All states hammerhead pontoon, hard, oyster sheds, fishing boats.
38. Oak Tree Creek: Top-of-tide. A secret garden of the Blackwater, dinghy.
39. Old Mill Creek: Top-of-tide creek behind the saltmarsh island of Mill Point, saltings.
40. Old Hall Creek: Most states lower down, but top-of-tide up past where the old barges would have docked, saltmarshes.
41. Peldon Creek: Top-of-tide, saltings and red hill.
42. Pennyhole Creek: Dammed, half-tide, saltings.
43. Ray Creek: Half-tide and up, countryside, Ray Island, Bonner's saltings.
44. Rolls Creek: High tide, red hills, beach.
45. Sales Point Creek: Small top-of-tide creek. Has a pill box and former Bradwell Bay airfield nearby, dinghy.

46. Salcott Creek: Yacht moorings, oyster layings, withies, and water most states in the channel, top of tide to get right up to the saltings and village.

47. Saltcote Creek: Ballast Hole, wharf, torpedo boat wreck and hulk. Top-of-tide.

48. Sampson's Creek: Dammed, top-of-tide creek. Hulk, saltings and nearby Feldy marshes.

49. Southey Creek: Top-of-tide to go over the 'Stakes' causeway, half tide lower down, mudflats and saltings.

50. Steeple Creek: Top-of-tide, saltings, marsh and farmland. Has also been known as Bay Creeks.

51. St Lawrence Creek: Called Robin Hood Creek or Robinsons by some fishermen. Half-tide to low water, mudflats. High tide into saltings or half tide and up into Bradwell Creek.

52. Strood Creek: High tide, saltings, Ray Island. Covers the road to Mersea at high water springs.

53. Stumble Drain: Low water, mud flats, wildfowl.

54. Syphon Creek: Small inlet in saltings, top-of-tide. Isambard Kingdom Brunel's water syphon was near here.

55. The Gut: Small low water creek that joins Mersea and Thornfleet Creek at low tide, mudflats.

56. Thirslet Creek: Is also known as Thistly Creek by fishermen. During the 18th and early 19th century, Thistly Hard was a busy rural dock. Revealed around half tide. Vast spit, withies, upper northern reach has best site in the river of a red hill set in the 'cant'. Visit Gore Saltings at the head of the creek around high water.

57. Thornfleet Creek: All states, moorings, packing shed, hulk.

58. Tollesbury Creek: Most states, leavings, The Nass mudflats. Name may have derived from ships once having to pay a 'toll' to come up the creek and 'bury', for a town.

59. Transit Creek: Low water, mudflats, dinghy.

60. Weymarks Creek: High tide, beach, dinghy.

61. Wilkin's Creek: Also known as Wager's Creek and Gardener's. High tide, saltings, ancient fishing trap, another excellent red hill site set in

the 'cant'. Famous jam makers organic fruits grown in nearby fields.

62. Woodrolfe Creek: Or 'Woodup', also known as Woodrope. Around half tide to get up to the hard or marina. Saltings, mudbirths and former Trinity lightship.

Deeps: Where the creeks converge at Mersea Quarters.
Wade Creek: Behind the seawall dam in Ramsey Marshes.
Hoefleet Creek: Behind the seawall dam in the South Channel at Tollesbury Wick Marshes.

Johnny's Creek. The creek carves into the saltings where it is fun to navigate but a little tricky drying out. A wide section of the creek at its start from Bowles Creek has flat drying ground close in.

Enjoying a sail to the head of Copt Hall Creek.

This length of a smack's bulwark has been used as a concrete former when building one of the old boat sheds beside Bontin's Creek in Tollesbury. The letters CK and two numbers are upside down but can just be made out. The groove in the board dispels any doubt that it was once part of a smack; possibly one of the eighty or so that would have worked up and down the local creeks during the heyday of working sail.

Just above Heybridge Basin lay the two hulks of Charles Burley *and* Lady Helen. *Beside them are concrete pillars at Metes Hard. The pillars appear to be out of place but over the seawall is a former gravel works, now an inland lake and nature reserve.*

Dinghies still manage to get in the delightful Hove Creek.

Bulham beach. At the easternmost of two small areas along this spit of sand and shingle, it is possible for the shoalest of keels to pass from the main river into Bulham Creek, or vice versa, at high tide. The lonely beach hut idyll has its own private beach.

The tiny Oak Tree Creek fills at the top of spring tide, and can be found when exploring close in along the southern shoreline of Osea Island. The small waterway is almost impossible to see when out in the river.

The Causeway, a mile long tidal road built by Romans to reach the fertile ground of Osea Island. Spanning the north side of the river it becomes visible from around half tide. Fishermen named this ancient road The Hard.

Larnch Creek. One of the low water creeks. The creek passes under the Osea causeway winding southeast through the mudflats until it joins Ford Creek. Small flocks of terns can be observed dive-bombing for fish along this shallow creek.

One of the great joys of small-boat cruising is being able to reach the most unlikely of places. Here there is just enough water to pole along this narrow cut through dense saltmarsh.

Concrete pillboxes dot the shores of the river on both sides up to Osea Island. The wartime structures offer more opportunities for exploring as well as making useful landmarks or bearings.

Thames sailing barge Dawn, *built in 1897 at Maldon. She was relaunched in 2007 after a full refurbishment at Heybridge.* Dawn *can often be seen at the pile moorings in Ray Creek, and is a magnificent example of a stack barge.*

Daybreak over Lawling Creek.

Miscellaneous Distances.

Approximate length of creek	Distance from Goldhanger to
Thirslet 2 nm	Joyce's Creek 0.5 nm
Goldhanger 1.8 nm	Osea Island/ Bawley Creek 1 nm
Mell 0.3 nm	East Point, Osea 1.5 nm
St Lawrence 1 nm	Rolls Creek 2.2nm
Bradwell 1.1 nm	Wilkin's Creek 0.75 nm
Lawling 1.9 nm	Awl Creek 2 nm
Mayland 1 nm	Hilly Pool Point 2.2 nm
Old Hall 1 nm	Maldon Hythe 4 nm
Woodrolfe 0.6 nm	Steeple Creek 2.6 nm
South Channel, Tollesbury 1.1 nm	Bradwell Creek (Baffle) 5.5 nm
Little Ditch 1.4 nm	Sales Point lighters (wavebreak) 7.5 nm
Salcott (Quarters to church) 3.5 nm	Gunner's Creek 8.2 nm
Ray 1 nm	Mersea Quarters 6.3 nm
Death 0.6 nm	The Stone 2.5 nm
Herring Point to The Hythe Maldon 1 nm	Circumnavigate Osea Island 5 nm

Acknowledgements

Researching for this book has not only provided me with the enjoyment gained from sailing to every creek on the River Blackwater, but it has also given me the opportunity to speak to many people up and down the length of the river. The added bonus has been that many of them have become good friends. Heartfelt gratitude goes to all who have shared their experiences with me, however small. In particular, Mike Newport, who helped capture the cover image, Brian Goodbourn, for his continual support, and Keith Jordan and Eustace King for their in depth local knowledge of Goldhanger and Salcott respectively.

Paul Drake was able to help with some of the Tollesbury creek names and Steve Hall, who over the last few years has generously shared his vast know-how of the workaday traditions surrounding the watery world of the River Blackwater.

Michael Emmett was able to help with two or three names up-river and thanks, too, to fellow creeksailors Doug Scurry and Ralph Merry, who I was able to compare notes with.

Guy Tickner, who cruised single-handed in his Scaffie dinghy until his 90th year, and who is sadly no longer with us, was also an inspiration.

Ian Barratt for his unstinting editing and Terry Smith at tfsmudgecreative for the cover design and artwork.

And to that incomparable icon of the shallow swatchways, Charles Stock, for inspiring me not only to seek adventure under sail in the forgotten creeks, but also to write about them.

And last but not least my family; Theresa, Harry, Hannah and Millie who, when not joining me afloat, allow one the freedom to pursue the all-consuming adventure that is Creeksailing . . .

Bibliography and Further Reading

Blackwater Men. Arthur and Michael Emmett
Coastal Adventure. J Wentworth Day
Down Tops'l. Hervey Benham
East Anglian Shores. David Fairhall
Essex Rivers And Creeks. Robert Simper
Last Stronghold Of Sail. Hervey Benham
Mehala. Sabine Baring-Gould
Open-Boat Cruising, Coastal and Inland Waters. Frank And Margaret Dye
Sailing Just For Fun. A C Stock
Sailing Tours Part 1, The Coasts Of Essex & Suffolk. Frank Cowper
Single Handed Yachtsman. F B Cooke
The Salty Shore. John Leather
The Voyage Alone in The Yawl Rob Roy. John Macgregor
Tide Time. A S Bennett
Tideways and Byways in Essex and Suffolk. Archie White
Waterside Memories. Frank Drake
Working Traditional Sail. Michael Emmett & Kevin Murphy

Websites
www.bargetrust.org
www.creeksailor.blogspot.com
www.essex-family-history.co.uk
www.essexheritagetrust.co.uk
www.itsaboutmaldon.co.uk
www.merseamuseum.org.uk
www.nauticalarchaeologysociety.org
www.sailingbargeassociation.co.uk
www.seax.essexcc.gov.uk
www.shipmate.org.uk
www.smackdock.co.uk
www.traditionalcharter.co.uk
www.unlockingessex.essexcc.gov.uk
www.visionofbritain.org.uk